Debbie & Jo

I pray th

to bless your marriage & that

that He will give you His very best as you seek this together.

Pastor Glen Townsend
Feb 4, 2018

Secret Space

30-Day Devotional & Workbook for Couples Seeking God's Best for Their Marriage

NNUS Publishing House

NNUS Publishing House

Secret Space

30-Day Devotional & Workbook for Couples Seeking God's Best for Their Marriage

Ghia Townsend

With

Cynthia Grenyion
Veron Modest
Melissa Nunes

NNUS Publishing House

Published by NNUS Publishing House: Nothing is New Under the Sun
located in Brampton, Ontario, Canada

Requests to book Professor Ghia Townsend for Workshops, Seminars and Conferences should be addressed to TownsendMCCC@gmail.com

Cover Design: Professor Ghia Townsend
Artwork: Mrs. Carolyn Soldano

First Edition: January 2018
Printed in the United States of America

ISBN: 978-1-7752378-0-8

NNUS Publishing House

Dedication

To my Heavenly Father, Constant Companion, Teacher, Counsellor, Lord, Saviour and Friend, and to my beautiful husband, best friend and greatest supporter. G.T.

To my beloved husband, who celebrates my accomplishments and encourages me to be the best of me. C. G.

To my amazing husband and beloved son, whose love is God's gift to me. V. M.

To my darling husband and number one cheerleader, and to my beautiful children. M. N.

"I was challenged to write about marriage from a place of both strength and weakness." p. xiii-xiv

I had continued to pursue happiness and to hurt my husband and I was determined to dissolve the marriage until God finally intervened. p. 3

"Unknown to me during those tender moments with God, he was already meeting me at my point of need. After I stepped out in faith by telling my Heavenly Father that I would honor my marriage covenant by choosing to stay with my husband out of obedience to Him, His unmistakable presence in my life became even more evident." p. 4

"God's heart was continually extended to me after our conversation that night and He endued me with courage to take the next inevitable steps." p. 5

About the Author

Professor Ghia Townsend, MSc. C. Psych. Assoc. is a Professor of Psychology and Counselling in the Department of Christian Counselling at Canada Christian College and School of Graduate Theological Studies. She is a Registered Member of the College of Psychologists of Ontario and the Newfoundland and Labrador Psychology Board, licensed to practice Counselling and Clinical Psychology with Adolescents, Adults, Couples and Families.

Professor Townsend is the Director and Clinical Supervisor at Townsend Marriage and Christian Counseling Center (TMCCC), a Christian Ministry that focuses extensively on the healing and restoration of Marriages by integrating Psychological Research and Clinical Practice with Biblical Principles and Prayer. Townsend Marriage and Christian Counseling Center is a Division of Canadian Psychology and Counseling Center Co. Ltd. (CPCC).

Professor Townsend is a Dynamic Motivational Speaker and Teacher; Gifted Author and Songwriter; Anointed Singer/Worship Leader and Lead Singer of the Band, Edge of Reason.

Professor Townsend lives in Ontario, Canada with her husband, Dr. Norman Townsend, Jnr. and her sons, Norman Townsend, III and Nathan Townsend.

Table of Contents

Acknowledgement

I am thankful to my Heavenly Father for the completion of this book and for showing me daily that truly, I can do all things through Jesus Christ who gives me strength. Like the Apostle Paul, I have learned to boast in my weaknesses because I have come to appreciate them as opportunities to experience Christ's power being perfected in my weaknesses. I am especially grateful to the Holy Spirit, who has been my Friend, Teacher, and Constant Companion, guiding me in my daily affairs as well as through the process of writing and publishing this book. Lord Jesus Christ, you are my Saviour and I am eternally grateful that your sacrifice on the cross at Calvary, now allows me to live a life filled with meaning and purpose as I press towards the mark for the prize of the high calling of God.

I express heartfelt gratitude to my beautiful husband, Dr. Norman Townsend, Jnr. Norman, you are one of my greatest blessings from God. After 17 years, you are still the kindest, most patient, supportive, and understanding person I know. You truly are beautiful and I grow to love you more with each year that passes. Thank you for being submitted to God and for being obedient to the leading of the Holy Spirit in our marriage, family and home.

I am deeply appreciative of my mother-in-law, Eugennie Lewis. Mom, you are my role model; a woman of prayer and purpose who taught me how to fight my battles on my knees. Thank you for believing in me and for loving me through the tough "Prodigal" years.

I take this time to express my sincere gratitude to individuals whom God placed in my life as leaders, mentors, teachers, counsellors, supervisors, and surrogate mothers, fathers, sisters and brothers; Pastor Tony Soldano and Mrs. Carolyn Soldano, Pastor Audrene Kerr-Brown and Pastor Leighton Brown, Pastor Veronica Rowe and Rev. Dr. Garth Rowe, Dr. Jennifer Martin, Mrs. Sonia Bryson, Mrs. Caryl Moorman, Rev. Dr. Philip Robinson, Ms. Theresa Coderre, Ms. Jancy King, Mr. James Walsh, Nurse Jerry Lowe-James, Dr. Adrienne Eastwood, Ms. Vellonic Brown, Dr. Sasha Turner-Bryson, Ms. Pamella Brown, Ms. Emuesiri Medu, Ms. Nakiema Palmer, Dr. Roxan Richards-Johnson, Dr. Shelley Henry-McKenzie, Ms. Candace Paddock, Dr. Terry Diamond, Dr. Shelley Gorman and Dr. Robert Stevens. Each of you has played a unique and indispensable role in shaping me into the woman I am today.

Preface

The Holy Spirit instructed me to write a 30-Day Devotional for Christian Married Couples one month ago. I anticipated that this task would be challenging and would require a substantial time investment, but I agreed and I started writing immediately. I also persisted with the task although it became increasingly evident that; God required more depth in each chapter than I had initially realized; He was not concerned about my time constraints and He wanted the book written in two weeks.

The book began to take shape when the Holy Spirit revealed the title of each chapter and the format of each entry. Next, He instructed me to extend an invitation to partner with three women I had taught at Canada Christian College and School of Graduate Theological Studies. Cynthia Grenyion's input in the writing of the beautiful prayers in the book was remarkable. Likewise, Veron Modest, and Melissa Nunes' support and contribution to the writing of prayers and assignments respectively were invaluable.

Writing this book was challenging in many other ways: I was challenged to write about marriage from a place of both strength and weakness; I was challenged to rely on God's revelation to develop the chapters; I was further challenged to write from a place that was personal and therefore, easy for readers to relate to; Yet, I was also expected to maintain a level of distance throughout the book that would allow readers to focus on God and allow the Holy Spirit to work in their hearts.

The process of writing the book was a delightful and refreshing experience for each of us and I am humbled by the way in which God has ministered to our hearts concerning our marriages during the hours dedicated to seeking him and writing. Additionally, I am excited about the work that God has started in the Couple's Ministry at Townsend Marriage and Christian Counseling Center and I pray that He will use this book in the process of restoring and blessing marriages across this nation and around the world.

Having seen the end of the process, I am pleased to say that I am happy that I took God at his word that we (myself with the support of Cynthia Grenyion, Veron Modest, and Melissa Nunes) could write this book in less than 96 hours. With man this is impossible but with God all things are possible. Having accomplished the goal, we have emerged from the process with a deeper appreciation for our husbands and the gift of marriage that God has given to each of us.

God cares about marriages. He demonstrates this daily in both my personal and professional life. Therefore, I encourage you to take the leap of faith required to begin this 30-day journey and to surrender your marriage to God because He is more than able to meet you at your point of need.

Couples are encouraged to complete the daily devotions together and in chronological order. Each day's Devotion includes: The passage of Scripture that is the focal point for the day; Reflections in which the author teaches concerning a specific aspect of marriage, and integrates the lesson with the passages of Scripture highlighted; Couple Enrichment Exercises that provide couples with an opportunity to practice what they have learned that day; and finally a written Prayer for the couple to petition God concerning their marriage based on the specific need identified in the Reflection and Couple Enrichment Exercises..

Resist the temptation to read ahead without carefully working through the recommended tasks while keeping in mind that the process is not intended to be rigid. Some couples will be able to complete 30 days within the designated timeframe. For others, this may not be suitable. Please pray for wisdom to determine what would be best for your marriage based on your unique circumstances.

It is highly recommended that you refrain from completing the journey in fewer than 30 days. Give yourselves time to;

reflect on what you have learned, evaluate your response to the lesson; and implement recommendations before moving on to the next day's Devotion. Finally, I pray that God will bless your marriage as you've determined in your hearts to seek and trust Him.

God Chose My Husband

God has blessed me beyond measure throughout my life and one of His greatest blessings to me is my husband, Norman whom God chose to be my husband. Norman has been in my life for over 17 years and I have seen firsthand what God can do in a marriage, where two people come to terms with the fact that they cannot do it on their own and surrender to His Will.

I had only recently begun attending a church on my University campus when I learned about God's will concerning my future husband. The Lead Pastor's wife had previously extended multiple invitations for me to attend a Sunday Service and I had graciously accepted her invitations without following through. To my surprise, she showed up at my residence unannounced months later and informed me she would not leave unless I accompanied her to church. Therefore, I finally followed through.

I had been visiting this church for a short time when a Prophetess ministering during the service called me to the altar and told me, "that young man [Norman] is the man God chose to be your husband". Therefore, I married Norman 4-years later in the University Chapel before God, our friends, and our family.

Two years into our marriage I could not bear the thought of being married for one more day. My heart yearned for more… I wanted excitement. I wanted romance. I wanted connection, and I could not make my marriage work, despite my best efforts. Not surprisingly, I began courting sin. With the advent of social media, it was easy to have an affair yet reason that I was not cheating because the relationship was not physical. I checked out of my marriage physically and emotionally and instead, chose to share my heart, my dreams and my desires with a man who was not my husband, but who promised to fill the void in my heart that my husband couldn't.

After nurturing this new relationship for months, it was clear what I had to do. I was not in love with my husband. I loved him, but I had never really been in love with him… I reasoned that I had the right to be happy. So I did the unthinkable: I told my husband our marriage was over; I asked him for a divorce, and I began the process of finding a new place to live.

Over the next few weeks, my heart became increasingly hardened towards my husband. There was nothing he could say to change my mind. I had tried everything within my power to connect with him during our two years of marriage and when that didn't work I pleaded and I cried to no avail. He was set in his ways and he did not accept that there was a problem in our marriage. I was angry with Norman and his efforts to save our marriage served only to push me further away and to increase the emotional connection I had developed with the other man.

I could not be reasoned with. Not by my friends, mother-in-law or my sisters. After all, how could they truly understand what it was like to be in my position? I believed that I finally had a chance to be happy.

I had continued to pursue happiness and to hurt my husband and I was determined to dissolve the marriage until God finally intervened. I had spent just over an hour talking to my "soul mate" on the telephone and was getting ready to go to bed when I heard the voice of God speak to me. In an unexpectedly gentle voice, the Holy Spirit said, "Ghia, this is the husband I chose for you. Will you continue to reject me?" I was caught off guard. When no one else could get through to me, God stepped out from behind the veil and commanded my obedience.

I was familiar with the voice of God, because during my early years of life, and especially after I was orphaned, he became a constant presence in my life: He revealed Himself as the God who was directing my path and orchestrating events to conform my life to His will. His voice was one I could not and was not prepared to disobey. When God spoke to me that night, I finally broke. My eyes were opened and I was confronted with the sin I had become desensitized to. I responded by falling on my knees before God in surrender to his will for my life. I acknowledged my sin before God and my husband. I repented. Then, I asked for forgiveness.

Following my encounter with the Spirit of God, I had no idea how I would move forward. I still did not love my husband and the feelings of passion for the other man had not diminished. Helplessly, I did the only thing I could think of. I approached God's Throne of Grace and I poured out my heart to him. I spoke honestly to the God that I had come to know as the unseen hand that was opening doors and working miracles in my life to advance my education and my career. I said to the Lord that night as I prayed, "Father, I do not love Norman and I don't know how to let go of the man that I am in love with." The thought of releasing this man was unbearable: The depth of grief, anguish, and pain I felt at the prospect of letting go was inconceivable, and I felt like I would die rather than live without him. However, God was not indifferent to my reality.

Unknown to me during those tender moments with God, he was already meeting me at my point of need. After I stepped out in faith by telling my Heavenly Father that I would honor my marriage covenant by choosing to stay with my husband out of obedience to Him, His unmistakable presence in my life became even more evident.

God's heart was continually extended to me after our conversation that night and He endued me with courage to take the next inevitable steps. I understood what I needed to do. Norman did not have a chance at winning my heart if I continued to nurture a relationship with another man. So I decided to terminate contact without notice. I chose not to accept any further phone calls. I chose to delete new text messages despite my desire to hear from him. I chose to block his emails. I chose to delete all contact details and I chose to delete my social media accounts. After taking these measures, I also commenced professional counselling with my husband.

The months that followed were tough, but it was evident that Norman had forgiven me. He never reminded me of what I did to him. His words and his actions remained consistent and his love proved to be unconditional. The manner in which Norman treated me was unexplainable. Except, I saw God's fingerprint on his heart.

I had not recognized it before, but when God chose this man to be my husband, He also placed His Agape love in his heart as He prepared him for life with a woman who was shattered on the inside. Prior to the months following my betrayal, I took that love for granted. Norman could not articulate why he loved me. Yet, I craved that validation. Most people in his position appeared to have a clear reason for the feelings they have toward their spouse. For example, I would listen with envy as other husbands talked about their wives, "I love her because... she is beautiful, articulate, funny, accomplished, disciplined" etcetera. This was not the case for Norman. He was a man of few words and he would simply respond, "I don't know why. I just do." In contrast, the man I fell in love with, despite not having ever met me in person, convincingly expressed his love with eloquence and passion that caused me to walk around dazed for days. I held on to his every word, and the excitement I felt as I waited for his messages was palpable. Unlike my husband, he was not hesitant to tell me the wonderful things I wanted... no, needed to hear and those words were enough to bandage the scars on my wounded heart.

I have since come to appreciate that Norman provided exactly what God intended for me to have in our marriage. With the exception of God, Norman was the first person who would not reject me, even when my actions warranted that response. His expectations of me were clear and he held me accountable for my actions. Additionally, my actions did not influence his love for me. He treated me with kindness at all times and asked for nothing in return.

This revelation was difficult for me to cope with because, unlike Norman who was consistent in his behaviour, principles, character, determination, and his resolve, I was like a leaf being tossed to and fro by the wind. He was consistent in carrying out his responsibilities in all areas of his life; I struggled in every area of mine. Furthermore, I did not possess the same capacity for love: I needed acknowledgement and validation or I would withhold my affection.

I was seldom unaware of my struggles and weaknesses, and I carried a deep sense of shame and guilt, especially following my affair. I felt like I imagine Gomer must have felt next to Hosea, being a woman scorned. However, I also understood that God had a purpose for choosing Norman to be my husband. God has used my husband, in His Refining Process, to shape me into the woman that I am today.

I did not fall in love with Norman immediately as I had hoped, but as the years passed, by God's grace, I grew to love him unconditionally and to respect him. Having put the affair behind us and settled back into a predictable routine, I was again confronted with the feelings of emptiness that had slowly crept back into my heart. This was not surprising because people who are broken are constantly searching for ways to fill the void in their heart. I needed someone… I needed something… I needed anything to dull the gnawing that made me feel restless and bored.

I began to view my husband as a perfect person and in doing so began to idolize him. I trusted his word above anyone else's and he could do no wrong in my eyes. I put my husband up on a pedestal while continuing to view myself as unworthy next to him. Norman was unbelievably smart (Ph.D. in Chemistry at age 25 and a National Chess champion). He was incredibly athletic (MVP athlete in track and field, soccer, cricket, volleyball, basketball and, badminton). On top of this, he was wise, humble and reserved, yet charismatic and sociable. I was enamoured with my husband and it did not take long for me to elevate him to the place in my heart that was meant for God.

Our marriage as the years passed improved considerably and my commitment to the marriage became more firm. I had both feet inside my marriage door and I was no longer yearning for more. Even so, I could not shake the persistent sense of knowing that something was not quite right. I was beginning to question my husband's fidelity but felt extremely reluctant to even consider the possibility that he could ever break his vows. Therefore, I responded by dismissing the thought I believed was evidence of my personal insecurities. If I dared to ask him about it, his gentle response, "no" was sufficient for me.

I had spent most of my life following the leading of the Holy Spirit, but I did not recognize for years that He was responsible for the unexplainable knowledge I had concerning my husband's fidelity. God was alerting me to the fact that something was amiss in my marriage. My husband had taken God's place in my heart and my husband's "friend" was too close to his heart. When I persisted in ignoring the signs, the Lord intervened in other ways; allowing evidence to emerge unexpectedly.

When I eventually realized that the friendship was a threat to my marriage, I took matters into my hands by forcing my husband to choose between his friend and his family. He protested that his relationship was innocent but nonetheless agreed to release this woman. This worked for a while, but we soon found ourselves in a perpetual cycle. No sooner would Norman and I begin to have challenges in our marriage than he would resume his friendship. Shortly afterwards, I would inevitably become aware of the phone calls, text messages and or emails. I would respond by confronting them, prompting her disappearance for a year or two until we began struggling again in our marriage.

This went on for 11 years until God decided it was enough. On the last occasion when she initiated contact with my husband, the Holy Spirit alerted me to a message she had sent two hours earlier. I was exasperated and in my frustration, I began responding to her message when the Holy Spirit said, “I thought you said you would let me take control of your marriage”. I let go of the reigns that day and God responded instantaneously by breaking the bond that existed between my husband and his friend. That was the last time they communicated with each other.

God was fighting for my marriage and I surrendered my heart to him. I was no longer expecting my husband to make me happy. I was happy. Jesus Christ became the center of my life and I began to seek after God with all my heart. This, however, was only the beginning because God was not finished working on our marriage.

Nine years had passed since I submitted to God and chose to stay married to my husband when the Holy Spirit began prompting me to invite my husband into the Secret Space I shared with God. I got used to fighting my battles on my knees by spending hours in my physical closet praying. I needed this time with God. It refreshed me and I looked forward to every moment reading the word, praising, praying and talking to my Heavenly Father. So when God said, "Invite your husband to join you in Our Secret Space", I did not want to share that part of my life with Norman. I cherished my time in God's presence and I did not know how to let my husband into that space. It took almost one week for me to submit to the Spirit of God, but eventually relented and asked Norman to join me. What happened next was unexpected. We had been entering the closet to pray for three consecutive nights and had settled into a comfortable rhythm of praying with and for each other. We were also deliberate in inviting the Holy Spirit's participation in our conversations and we were becoming increasingly aware of His presence.

However, I had one more secret… and the Holy Spirit convicted me to share it with my husband. We were in a good place with each other, but that was not nearly good enough for God. We still had a wall between us that prevented us from being vulnerable with each other. Our hearts continued to be guarded and, therefore, we could not experience the passion that we both yearned for unless the invisible wall came down. When the Holy Spirit instructed me to tell Norman the secret I held on to, I was afraid. I had already hurt him beyond measure and I did not want to hurt him further. Yet, I knew that I could not willfully disobey God either. Therefore, I released the secret that had shackled my heart for years.

I told my husband that I called another man on our wedding day. This man was my choice for a husband, and I had loved him since I was 16-years old. I accepted Norman's marriage proposal out of obedience to God, even though I continued to love this man. This is the hardest thing I have ever had to tell my husband to date. As I sobbed uncontrollably, I told him that I had called this man, prior to our wedding, hoping he would ask me not to go through with our wedding. I also told him that I was saddened when this man blessed my marriage instead.

I had never felt more exposed in my life. My emotions were raw and there was nothing that I could do to rebuild the wall around my heart. I glanced up at Norman and noticed that he was not looking at me, but was shaking uncontrollably as he stared at his hands. We were both transfixed in the moment for what felt like hours until in a split second, his wall went back up and he pulled himself together. I was not prepared for his words to me, "G, let's go to bed." It was all I could do not to sink into the floor beneath me. As gently as I could muster, choking on my despair, I told him, "No". I was wounded. I felt betrayed and I was angry with God for exposing me as He had. After Norman exited the closet, I curled up on the floor and fell asleep until the Holy Spirit awakened me at approximately 2:00 AM, and prompted me to go to my husband. When I laid next to my husband, he simply reached out and held me as he always did before drifting back to sleep. I did not sleep for a moment. I stayed up all night thinking about how to protect my heart.

The following day, Norman asked if I would go on a date with him. I declined initially, fearing that the closeness would overwhelm me. However, I eventually relented and agreed to go for ice cream. This was acceptable. I reasoned that we would eat our ice cream then return home where I would hide in my closet. Norman, however, was not his usual self. No sooner had we entered our car than he started sharing that he had listened to a program on JOY 1250 - Hometown Christian Radio on his way to work that morning. He was so moved by this program that he recorded it with the intention of inviting me to listen to it with him. I did not like where this was going. He identified with the couple; a pastor and his wife who had neglected their marriage in the process of focusing all their efforts on their ministries.

Norman expressed to me that he felt as though he had not been the best husband that God has called him to be and it was his heart's desire to change. He was being vulnerable with me, for the first time, but I could not receive it because the pain from the night before still lingered in my heart. God, however, was not about to let me interfere with the work he was doing in our marriage. Without any preamble or warning, the Holy Spirit said to me, "Ask him the question you have been asking him for nine years." I was afraid to ask him, but I did because I also expected that he would tell me what I already knew. Without hesitation, my husband proceeded to confess his betrayals, not just with his "friend", but with another woman who was unknown to me at that time. I was frozen inside, but I handled myself as I would during a professional interview with a client. I was dispassionate. I asked for the facts, and I listened without interrupting him when he spoke. I suppose I would have continued in that manner, except God suddenly removed my defenses and allowed me to feel the full weight of the revelation.

After Norman completed his last statement, my shield of strength shattered and it gave way to inconsolable grief and despair, unlike anything I had ever experienced in my life despite having lived through the death of both my birth parents. Norman held me as I wailed uncontrollably, and I did not have the strength to push him away because I was too weak and too broken in that moment.

Even then, God was still not finished. When I managed to pull myself together, the Holy Spirit spoke again saying,

"Tell him you forgive him completely and that you surrender the RIGHT to hold him accountable for his sins against you." This was hard because I wanted to hurt him. I especially wanted to punish him for the years when I held him in high regard thinking he was better than I was. However, I did not get that satisfaction because God further reminded me that He forgave me after sending His Only Begotten Son, Jesus to die on a cross to pay the price for my sins. In like manner, "You must also forgive your husband the debt owed to you". Out of obedience to the Spirit of God, I told my husband that I forgave him and that I would never remind him of what he did or use it against him.

This was easier said than done and over the next week, following the disclosure, I spent hours crying and hurting over and over again. Even so, I accepted by faith that God would take the sting out of the memory of my husband's betrayal and would heal my broken heart.

God is faithful to his word, which once sent forth does not return void. He continues to work on my marriage piece by piece, shaping it with His own two hands, and He is determined to create a masterpiece that reveals His Glory.
God has called me to minister healing to others and, as I humble myself before Him, He uses me to heal countless marriages of the couples He brings to my office. Additionally, He watches over my marriage and He continues to intervene directly in order to keep it undefiled.

Day 1

His Throne of Grace

HEBREW 4: 14-16

14 Since then we have a great high priest who has passed through the heavens, Jesus, the Son of God, let us hold fast our confession. 15 For we do not have a high priest who is unable to sympathize with our weaknesses, but one who in every respect has been tempted as we are, yet without sin. 16 Let us then with confidence draw near to the throne of grace that we may receive mercy and find grace to help in time of need.

REFLECTION

As you embark on this journey together, consider that you are renewing your commitment to each other and making a new covenant with God. Your marriage is sacred and it is a gift to you from your Heavenly Father. To take your marriage and each other for granted is to dishonor the Giver of your gift.

Therefore, beginning a spiritual journey with each other is an opportunity for you to approach God's Throne of Grace in humility and to acknowledge his Lordship over your lives and your marriage. It is also an opportunity for you to understand that although you will face many challenges and temptations, Jesus has made a way for you to approach your Heavenly Father; to seek, and gain the help that is necessary to overcome every hurdle that lies ahead. There is nothing that you will not be able to overcome when you actively seek to put your relationship with each other in the hands of the One who knows you completely and is invested in your welfare.

COUPLE ENRICHMENT EXERCISE

Reflect on God's words to you, spoken in Hebrews 4: 16, as you go through your day; ask yourselves the following questions; then discuss your answers with each other:

- Who is Jesus Christ?
- What has he done for us?
- How does His sacrifice affect our lives?

- How does our relationship with Him affect our marriage?

PRAYER

Father, we acknowledge Your Lordship over our lives. We invite You to take Your rightful place in our hearts and in our Marriage. We let go of the reigns of our marriage and we ask for Your very best in our Marriage. In Jesus' name, we pray. Amen.

"There is nothing that you will not be able to overcome when you actively seek to put your relationship with each other in the hands of the One who knows you completely and is invested in your welfare." p. 16

Day 2

Lord, Show Me My Heart

MATTHEW 7: 4-5
4 Or how can you say to your brother, 'Let me take the speck out of your eye,' when there is the log in your own eye? 5 You hypocrite, first take the log out of your own eye, and then you will see clearly to take the speck out of your brother's eye.

REFLECTION
The word "hypocrite" from the above scripture may appear harsh to many persons. Yet, it is an appropriate criticism. The reality is that unless you are prepared to take an honest and critical look at yourselves and in so doing, humble yourselves before your Heavenly Father, this journey of Seeking God for His Best in your marriage will be an exercise in futility.

There is no one, with the exception of Jesus Christ, who is perfect. Do not roll your eyes. Yes, you are not perfect. You may be great at your job. Certainly, you do an amazing job with your children, with your home, with your finances… But, that still does not make you perfect. I'm deliberately belabouring this point and will not move on until you stop rolling your eyes or anything else you might be doing right now to avoid hearing the message behind these words.

Marriage is challenging as a whole, but becomes unnecessarily complex because partners lack empathy for each other. We automatically see the flaws in our spouse (i.e., the "speck" in their eyes) but we are unwilling or unable to see that we have a "log" in our own eyes. We all tend to judge ourselves less harshly than we do others and for that reason, we do not immediately recognize that our shortcomings, weaknesses, flaws, and errors are in fact equivalent to our spouse's in God's eyes.

Hebrews 4: 13 states that no creature is hidden from God's sight, but all are naked and exposed to the eyes of Him to whom we must give account. God knows exactly who you are and when you are willing to take an honest look at yourselves and ask Him to show you who you really are he will do so. This might be a fearsome thought, but be assured that when you seek God for His Best he will not destroy you. In other words, he will not give you a serpent when you ask him for fish (Matthew 7: 10).

COUPLE ENRICHMENT EXERCISE

Find a quiet place today and reflect on the devotion individually:

- Ask God to reveal three things about yourself that are undesirable in the context of your marriage.
- Ask God to create an opportunity for you to share these three things with each other in a manner that honours him.
- Later, sit together and simply take turns sharing with each other what God has revealed to you about yourself.
- Do not provide any feedback to each other. Simply thank each other for sharing then leave the matter in God's hands.

PRAYER

Father, we thank You for the privilege to come before You as Your children. We thank You for Your love, grace, and mercy towards us. We acknowledge You as our Lord and Savior, and thank You for Your presence in our lives. You are the all-knowing and omnipresent God from whom nothing is hidden. We call upon You Lord and we are grateful for Your mercy. We confess our sins before You, thank You for Your forgiveness, and ask that You help us to forgive each other. Help us to see each other through Your eyes with a heart of love and compassion. Help us to see our failures as room for You to work in and through us so that our marriage will glorify Your name. In Jesus' name, we pray. Amen.

"We all tend to judge ourselves less harshly than we do others and for that reason, we do not immediately recognize that our shortcomings, flaws, and errors are in fact equivalent to our spouse's in God's eyes." p. 20

Day 3

Cleanse Me

1 JOHN 1: 5-10

5 This message we have heard from him and proclaim to you, that God is light, and in him is no darkness at all. 6 If we say we have fellowship with him while we walk in darkness, we lie and do not practice the truth. 7 But if we walk in the light, as he is in the light, we have fellowship with one another, and the blood of Jesus his Son cleanses us from all sin. 8 If we say we have no sin, we deceive ourselves, and the truth is not in us. 9 If we confess our sins, he is faithful and just to forgive us our sins and to cleanse us from all unrighteousness. 10 If we say we have not sinned, we make him a liar, and his word is not in us.

REFLECTION

So, full disclosure… The first 10 days of this devotional will be rough. If you've played any sport, currently or in the past, then you know that the beginning is usually the hard part. You tend not be in great shape at the beginning and, therefore, everything hurts. You should also consider that if you persevere, you will eventually reap the benefits of your labour. In contrast, those who dropped out of the game are usually haunted by the, "I wonder where I would be today, if I hadn't…?" thoughts.

The same principle applies to your marriage. Seeking God's best is never comfortable, but staying the course is a sure way to ensure that he reveals his glory in you. Sin separates you from God and inevitably will separate you from each other. No one is without sin. In fact, now would be a good time to revisit the Reflection on Day 2: You are not perfect and therefore, you will make and have made mistakes. Some of these mistakes are more serious than others, but God is faithful and just to forgive your sins and to cleanse you from all unrighteousness. However, to be forgiven you must first acknowledge those sins.

COUPLE ENRICHMENT EXERCISE

Purpose in your heart to cast off the burden that you have been carrying for far too long. Set aside time today individually to:

- Identify the offence(s) you have committed.
- Acknowledge them before God.
- Ask for His forgiveness.

This process is an act of Faith. As you do this with sincerity, God will open the door to your partner's heart in order to allow you to acknowledge your sins against him/her then seek forgiveness so that you can both move forward in your marriage with the assurance that you have been cleansed.

PRAYER

Father, we thank You that we can come before You boldly for help in our in time of need. With a humble heart we empty ourselves before You, knowing that You are a loving, forgiving, and gracious God. We confess our sins before You Lord, holding to the truth of Your word that You are faithful to forgive us of all our sins and to cleanse us from all unrighteousness. We thank You for the cross. We thank You for the blood of Your Son Jesus Christ that was shed on Calvary to demonstrate Your love and grant us the right to be called Your children. We acknowledge Your presence in us, which convicts us of our sins so that we can repent and experience Your mercy each day. In Jesus' name, we pray. Amen.

"So, full disclosure… The first 10 days of this devotional will be rough. If you've played any sport, currently or in the past, then you know that the beginning is usually the hard part." p. 23

Day 4

Secret Space

PSALM 91: 1-4

1 He who dwells in the shelter of the Most High will abide in the shadow of the Almighty. 2 I will say to the Lord, "My refuge and my fortress, my God, in whom I trust." 3 For he will deliver you from the snare of the fowler and from the deadly pestilence. 4 He will cover you with his pinions, and under his wings you will find refuge; his faithfulness is a shield and buckler.

REFLECTION

It's time to take a breath. I meant that literally. Go on… inhale deeply… now let it out. Imagine that you are putting this book aside to really talk to God and each other without the author being present. Now is the time for you to really learn how to speak honestly about where you are right now. That is, learning to speak the truth openly and honestly in love.

I would like you to identify a place in your home that you could designate as your "Secret Space". The idea behind this Secret Space is that when you enter this space with each other, you are automatically saying; Almighty God, we desire to be under Your shadow. You are further saying, Lord You are our refuge and fortress and it's in You, rather than ourselves, that we place our trust.

This is a necessary step in the process because you need the supernatural covering of God to persevere, and to overcome the attacks of the adversary who is determined to destroy your marriage.

The "Secret Space" is a physical space in your home where you will go to have truthful conversations with each other and with God. Yes, I meant with God. If you recall, nothing is hidden from God (Hebrews 4: 13). When you become conscious of God's Omnipresence in your relationship, this also carries an added responsibility and commitment on your part to not just reverence God, but to refrain from dishonoring your spouse.

COUPLE ENRICHMENT EXERCISE

You will now take a moment to talk with each other about the rules that will govern your "Secret Space":

- Always begin by inviting the Holy Spirit to join in your conversation with each other
- Ask God to keep you accountable for your actions and your words as you engage with Him and with each other
- Always ask God to help you to see the best in each other especially when it becomes necessary to have challenging conversations
- Ask God to teach you how to be quick to hear, slow to speak, and slow to anger (James 1: 19)

PRAYER

Father, we thank You for who You are. We acknowledge You as our Lord and Saviour and we praise You for what You are doing in our lives as individuals, and also as a couple. It is our desire to serve You, Lord. Therefore, we invite You to be with us as we commune with each other. Father, we are imperfect and as such, tend to fall short in our commitment to each other and to You. We know, however, that we are able to come to You for help; Father, grant us strength. Sustain us, equip us, renew us and refresh us each day. Lord, keep our hearts pliable so that we will see our need for change without becoming resentful and bitter. Teach us to listen to each other and to hear what's in each other's heart. Help us to remember Your love and compassion towards us, and to be loving and compassionate towards each other. As we set aside this place, as our "Secret Space", we ask for Your blessing and favour to open the door to truth and love. Let it be, in accordance with Your will, a place where honesty dwells and where our joy is evident. In Jesus' name, we pray, Amen.

Now is the time for you to really learn how to speak honestly about where you are right now. That is, learning to speak the truth openly and honestly in love. p. 27

Day 5

Lord, We Offer Up Our Marriage to You

GENESIS 22: 1-2

1 Some time later God tested Abraham. He said to him, "Abraham!" "Here I am," he replied. 2 Then God said, "Take your son, your only son, whom you love—Isaac—and go to the region of Moriah. Sacrifice him there as a burnt offering on a mountain I will show you."

REFLECTION

Abraham was instructed to place his son Isaac on the sacrificial altar. Put yourselves in Abraham's position for a moment. God promises you a child, fulfills his promise to you by giving you the child, but then instructs you to place your child on the altar as a living sacrifice.

I do not know any person who would not be mortified faced with the same situation. However, if you've read these scriptures you would have recognized that the purpose was to test whether the gift given was an idol that would inevitably separate Abraham from God.

Marriage is a covenant relationship ordained by God. Yet, by excluding God from your marriage you are essentially courting idolatry as would have been the case had Abraham refused to surrender his son to God. In contrast, by offering up your marriage as a living sacrifice to God, you are saying Lord, I place you first and I will not withhold what belongs to you. You are saying further, God within the context of our marriage, you are the third strand of the threefold cord that is not easily broken (Ecclesiastes 12:12).

COUPLE ENRICHMENT EXERCISE

Ask yourselves and each other the following questions and reflect on the responses that you share:

- What would our marriage look like if we sacrificed it on God's altar?
- How would we begin the process of letting go and allowing God to take control?
- When will we start?

PRAYER

Father, we thank You for Your love and faithfulness towards us. We acknowledge You as our Savior, our Guide, our Helper, our Protector, our Shield, and our Provider. All that we need can be found in You. We thank You for keeping our marriage as we choose to invite You into it. We know that we are unable to keep it flourishing, as it was meant to be, without You. Therefore, we commit it to You. Teach us to humble ourselves before You. Father, You brought us together and we are trusting You to sustain our marriage for Your glory and honor. In Jesus' name, we pray, Amen.

Day 6

We Choose to Follow Jesus' Example

EPHESIANS 5: 22-33

22 Wives, submit to your own husbands, as to the Lord. 23
For the husband is the head of the wife even as Christ is the
head of the church, his body, and is himself its Savior. 24
Now as the church submits to Christ, so also wives should
submit in everything to their husbands. 25 Husbands, love
your wives, as Christ loved the church and gave himself up
for her, 26 that he might sanctify her, having cleansed her
by the washing of water with the word, 27 so that he might
present the church to himself in splendor, without spot or
wrinkle or any such thing, that she might be holy and
without blemish. 28 In the same way husbands should love
their wives as their own bodies. He who loves his wife
loves himself. 29 For no one ever hated his own flesh, but
nourishes and cherishes it, just as Christ does the church,
30 because we are members of his body. 31 “Therefore a
man shall leave his father and mother and hold fast to his
wife, and the two shall become one flesh.” 32 This mystery
is profound, and I am saying that it refers to Christ and the
church. 33 However, let each one of you love his wife as
himself, and let the wife see that she respects her husband.

REFLECTION

The relationship between Jesus and the Church is a model for the relationship that God ordained between husbands and their wives. The scriptures referenced can be viewed as a blueprint for marriages. When God ordained the marriage union, He intended for it to be a relationship in which a woman submits to her husband's authority and demonstrates respect for him in both words and deeds. Of equal importance, men are called to love their wives, and to cherish and nurture them as they would their own bodies.

The Church is ultimately under the authority of Jesus Christ, its Lord and Savior, and is expected to submit to His ultimate authority. As the husband of the Church, Christ loved her so much that he gave up his own life for her. Romans 5: 7-8 tells us that one will scarcely die for a righteous person – though perhaps for a good person would dare even die – but God shows his love for us in that while we were still sinners, Christ died for us. The love that Jesus demonstrated was not earned by the Church and was not determined by His emotions. Instead, Jesus Christ gave His love freely and completely when He died on the cross to pay the price for our sins, and He did so although we did not deserve mercy.

The love that God ordained in marriage was fashioned after the example demonstrated by Christ. Therefore, a husband is called to love his wife in spite of himself. Although his emotions will inevitably ebb and flow, God expects him to be consistent in the manner in which he treats his wife and seeks to act in her best interests even when it is not earned or even deserved.

Similarly, a husband's leadership role within the context of marriage is a spiritual appointment and is therefore not dependent on his financial capacity, personality or any other attributes that could make him more or less worthy of his wife's respect.

Of course, it is never easy for a husband to love a wife who is selfish, self-centered and disrespectful. Neither is it easy for a wife to respect a husband who is mean-spirited, dogmatic and unloving. Therefore, I will hasten to say that with man (woman), the example set by Christ is impossible (Matthew 19: 26). The reality is that no one could reasonably expect to walk in obedience to these scriptures solely on the basis of their will-power or other personal attributes, but the good news is that we don't. Let's consider the second part of the scripture in Matthew 19: 26 that states, but with God all things are possible.

As couples who have purposed in your heart to seek God's best for your marriage, you will ultimately come to the realization that it is through the Spirit of God working in you and through you, and filling you that you will come to a place where you consistently place the needs and wellbeing of your spouse above your own needs and wellbeing.

COUPLE ENRICHMENT EXERCISE

Invite the Holy Spirit to join you in your Secret Space.

After you've settled in:

Wives:

- Ask your husband to share with you honestly the areas in your marriage where he believes you've struggled with submitting to him.
- Listen carefully to what he shares without interrupting even though you may likely disagree with him.
- Refrain from interrupting him as he speaks, but take a moment to write his responses to you.
- You should not argue with him concerning what he has shared. Instead, accept the feedback and, later, revisit what you have written in order to pray to God about it.
- Ask that God's will to be done in relation to what your husband expressed.

Husbands:

- Ask your wife to share with you honestly the areas in your marriage where she believes you've struggled with demonstrating Christ-like love towards her.
- Listen carefully to what she shares, without interrupting even though you may likely disagree with her.

- Refrain from interrupting her as she speaks, but take a moment to write her responses to you.
- You should not argue with her concerning what she has shared. Instead, accept the feedback and, later, revisit what you have written in order to pray to God about it. Ask that God's will be done in relation to what your wife expressed.

PRAYER

Father, we look to You because You are our example of love. You love us in spite of our faults. You provide for us even when we do not deserve it. Father, help us to submit to each other and to love each other wholeheartedly. Let Your love flow through us and give us faith to trust You to do the impossible things in our lives, and our marriage. In Jesus' name, we pray, Amen.

> Of course, it is never easy for a husband to love a wife who is selfish, self-centered and disrespectful. Neither is it easy for a wife to respect a husband who is mean-spirited, dogmatic and unloving. p. 35

Day 7

Lord, Break Our Walls Down

1 PETER 2:21-25

21 For to this you have been called, because Christ also suffered for you, leaving you an example, so that you might follow in his steps. 22 He committed no sin, neither was deceit found in his mouth. 23 When he was reviled, he did not revile in return; when he suffered, he did not threaten, but continued entrusting himself to him who judges justly. 24 He himself bore our sins in his body on the tree, that we might die to sin and live to righteousness. By his wounds you have been healed. 25 For you were straying like sheep, but have now returned to the Shepherd and Overseer of your souls.

REFLECTION

Marriages cannot thrive in an atmosphere where partners are in bondage. Yet, many couples enter marriage with baggage from the past. Baggage has many faces: For some, it's the wound from a previous relationship; for others, it sexual sins, addictions, pride and other character or integrity issues etcetera. The list is far too vast to reveal. Nonetheless, baggage leads to bondage that, irrespective of the manifestation, serves the purpose of erecting walls between a husband and his wife.

In order for couples to have a healthy relationship with each other, they must each possess the capacity to form a secure attachment bond. That is, they must have a desire for connection and also feel a sense of safety and security that allows them to pursue and maintain this connection. Unfortunately, although this need for closeness is innate, its expression is thwarted in many individuals, and manifests itself in many destructive ways in marriages.

Consider the spouse that is so jealous that his partner no longer has the freedom to go to the grocery store without being checked on repeatedly and bombarded with questions about who, what, when, where, why or how. A marriage cannot flourish under such conditions. Neither can a marriage thrive under conditions where one partner consistently rejects the sexual advances of the other, choosing to unfairly pathologize a healthy God-given desire for physical/ emotional closeness and pleasure.

The reality of the possibilities that could be highlighted is beyond the scope of this chapter. However, at the heart of the matter is the fact that marriages commence with great potential, but tend to shrink to a mere counterfeit of God's Best.

Today you are faced with a critical choice. Will you settle for “this is as good as it gets” or will you dare to believe God for more? God’s hands are not shortened that they cannot save your marriage. Neither are his ears dull, that they cannot hear when you cry out to him to heal your wounded hearts (Isaiah 59:1).

Your time for healing is now. For far too long you have been shackled by your past and weighed down by feelings of guilt, shame, fears, anxiety, and the insecurities that are unseen by the naked eye. This has kept you from expecting God’s best for your marriage and has caused you to settle. Stand in God’s presence with each other, and accept His gift to you: “By Jesus’s Stripes, you are healed”.

COUPLE ENRICHMENT EXERCISE

It's time to dig deeper. You have a reasonable idea about the past hurts and problems that still linger in your mind and continue to cripple your ability to bond with your spouse. This will be a challenging exercise for you, so I encourage you to enter your Secret Space together. You will do this exercise with each other, even though the focus will be on the partner who has the unresolved issue(s). It’s important that you each learn how to support each other emotionally. For example, allow your spouse to hold you as you go through this process, even though your instinct might be to push them away so you can escape the vulnerability that accompanies the process.

- Close your eyes and begin to talk to God about what has hurt you, even if your spouse is the person who hurt you in the past.
- As you do so, ask the Holy Spirit to fill you, and to heal your wounded heart.
- This exercise will be more challenging for your spouse if they were personally responsible for the hurt you now feel.
- Depending on the nature of the hurt and the current risk, you are strongly encouraged to seek professional counselling services in order to gain the necessary support that you will need: This book is not a substitute for professional intervention.

PRAYER

Father, we admit that our baggage is heavy. The weight of it is overwhelming, and it is a barrier between us. We desire harmony in our marriage and we desire to cast off our burdens in exchange for Your yoke that is easy and Your burden that is light. You are the only one who can release us from the weight of sin so that we will have the liberty to be intimate with each other, and to enjoy the pleasures that you have given to us. Father, we thank you for your healing today. In Jesus' name, we pray. Amen.

Day 8

Your Grace is Sufficient

2 CORINTHIANS 12:7-10

7 So to keep me from becoming conceited because of the surpassing greatness of the revelations, a thorn was given me in the flesh, a messenger of Satan to harass me, to keep me from becoming conceited. 8 Three times I pleaded with the Lord about this, that it should leave me. 9 But he said to me, "My grace is sufficient for you, for my power is made perfect in weakness." Therefore I will boast all the more gladly of my weaknesses, so that the power of Christ may rest upon me. 10 For the sake of Christ, then, I am content with weaknesses, insults, hardships, persecutions, and calamities. For when I am weak, then I am strong.

REFLECTION

The human heart is a harbour for pride. We all have the capacity to become conceited and proud. Before you start nodding your head as you are able to identify a friend, neighbour or colleague who is proud, and needs to humble himself/herself, please consider that no sooner had we begun to focus on how humble we are than we are, in fact, demonstrating the opposite. Stated differently, elevating ourselves above others whom we perceive to be proud is evidence of our pride.

Marriages tend to be saturated with pride: Are you constantly comparing yourself to your wife? Are you constantly refusing to acknowledge the extent to which your husband's contribution in the home adds value to your life, and to your children's wellbeing? Are you habitually watching to see whether your wife will follow your recommendation immediately and/or exactly as you've suggested? Are you deliberately withholding your affection because your wife nags you? Are you quietly seething that your husband lacks ambition? The next one is unbelievable… wait for it, are you angry that your husband is holding you back in life because God has deposited so much more in you than in him. Yikes! Now I'm really in trouble with you. It's a good thing that I'm still under the covering of my earlier disclaimer, "the first ten days will be tough".

Proverbs 8:13 states, the fear of the LORD is hatred of evil; Pride and arrogance and the way of evil and perverted speech I hate. Two years ago as I pondered what it means to be proud of heart, I asked the Holy Spirit what God means when he repeatedly says, "Humble yourself before me". In response to my question, the Holy Spirit drew my attention to Jeremiah 1: 5, "Before I formed you in the womb I knew you, and before you were born I consecrated you; I appointed you a prophet to the nations". While we are not all called to be prophets to the nations, as some of us are alternately called to be teachers, counsellors, bankers, police officers etcetera, the fact remains that it is God who apportions to each of us the gifts, abilities, and intellect that we now boast about.

Let's put it another way: You look down on your husband’s weaknesses as a slothful steward of your family’s financial resources on the basis that you are better able to manage your financial affairs. Yet, true humility is found in a heart that recognizes that God could just as easily have reversed the gifts. That is, you are the spendthrift of the family while your husband is the wise steward. The problem with this reversal, however, might likely be rather than recognize God’s grace, your husband becomes the one who alternately looks down on you in his own conceit.

How then does God choose to rectify this problem? He blesses you both with weaknesses as well as strengths and in his manifold wisdom, and grace he pairs you with a partner who is, in fact, your ideal helpmate possessing complimentary characteristics and attributes.

I would further like you to consider the Apostle Paul. God gave him a significant weakness (i.e., a thorn in his flesh) along with Spiritual gifts and revelations. Paul reasoned that God gave him this thorn in the flesh to keep him from becoming arrogant. This weakness, arguably, also kept him in a state of dependence on his Heavenly Father. Within the context of marriage, God's grace is available and is more than sufficient. For many couples who are challenged beyond their human capacity, God's hands are extended to you in this moment. Humble yourselves before the Almighty and submit yourselves one to another out of reverence for Christ (Ephesians 5: 21). In so doing, you will begin to recognize that your weaknesses are meant to remind you that you are ultimately dependent on God's all-sufficient Grace.

COUPLE ENRICHMENT EXERCISE

Today you will each create a list. Carry a sheet of paper with two columns: My Wife/Husband's Strengths; and My Weaknesses. Record the personal examples that the Holy Spirit brings to your awareness. At the end of your day, you will do the following:

- Place your lists on a table side by side then review them together. Pay attention to the degree to which your strengths and weaknesses are complimentary.
- Afterwards, engage in a conversation about how your differences could be harnessed to advance your marriage.

PRAYER

Father, we come to You recognizing and acknowledging Your all sufficient grace. May Your love and grace cover us so that we begin to use our combined strengths to solve the daily problems we encounter. Help us to see ourselves objectively, by viewing our differences from Your perspective, and by humbling ourselves before You and each other. Father, please forgive us for looking at our achievements as ours when truly they originated with You. Teach us how to view our weaknesses as opportunities to draw closer to You and to depend on you continuously. Regarding our strengths, Father we ask you to teach us how to use them to bless each other so that our marriage will bring glory and honor to you. In Jesus' name, we pray. Amen.

How then does God choose to rectify this problem? He blesses you both with weaknesses as well as strengths and in his manifold wisdom, and grace he pairs you with a partner who is, in fact, your ideal helpmate possessing complimentary characteristics and attributes. p. 45

Day 9

Fill My Cup and Let it Overflow

JOHN 4: 1-15

4 Now when Jesus learned that the Pharisees had heard that Jesus was making and baptizing more disciples than John 2 (although Jesus himself did not baptize, but only his disciples), 3 he left Judea and departed again for Galilee. 4 And he had to pass through Samaria. 5 So he came to a town of Samaria called Sychar, near the field that Jacob had given to his son Joseph. 6 Jacob's well was there; so Jesus, wearied as he was from his journey, was sitting beside the well. It was about the sixth hour.

7 A woman from Samaria came to draw water. Jesus said to her, "Give me a drink."8 (For his disciples had gone away into the city to buy food.) 9 The Samaritan woman said to him, "How is it that you, a Jew, ask for a drink from me, a woman of Samaria?" (For Jews have no dealings with Samaritans.) 10 Jesus answered her, "If you knew the gift of God, and who it is that is saying to you, 'Give me a drink,' you would have asked him, and he would have given you living water." 11 The woman said to him, "Sir, you have nothing to draw water with, and the well is deep. Where do you get that living water? 12 Are you greater

than our father Jacob? He gave us the well and drank from it himself, as did his sons and his livestock." 13 Jesus said to her, "Everyone who drinks of this water will be thirsty again, 14 but whoever drinks of the water that I will give him will never be thirsty again. The water that I will give him will become in him a spring of water welling up to eternal life." 15 The woman said to him, "Sir, give me this water, so that I will not be thirsty or have to come here to draw water."

REFLECTION

Cars are beautiful! I especially like luxury cars fully-loaded with all the bells and whistles and modern features for our ultimate convenience. Yet irrespective of their make, a car that is not well maintained will ultimately fail to maintain peak performance. Imagine for a moment that you are a Mercedes Benz... or a Maserati, if your mind can conceive it. Your oil indicator comes on alerting you to take the car in for regular oil change. However, you are super busy and therefore, you delay taking the car in for a few weeks reasoning that when the indicator first appeared your oil was at minimum 15% so you have a bit of time before it is depleted. Therefore, you continue to drive to work, take the kids to their activities and shop for your household. Time eludes you passing more quickly than you realized and still the oil levels have not been replenished.

God designed us with Bells and Whistles too. They are called emotions (smile). Did you notice how tired you've been feeling lately? Oops, sorry that was two weeks ago when the metaphorical oil indicator first appeared. You are now way beyond tired. Stress, anxiety, anger are all progressive states of the initial condition that you are yet to address. Having failed to take the car in for its scheduled maintenance, you've inadvertently forced it to operate under less ideal conditions and now, to your surprise it is not just your oil indicator that's flashing. Oh no… not the brake lights too! My goodness, you did not realize that your new car is defective. How can the engine light be flashing so soon?

It is okay to challenge my exaggeration. Yet, this is exactly the condition that we attempt to function in on a daily basis. If you are constantly operating in a deficient and unmaintained state you are in no position to nurture your spouse and family over the long term that life demands.

When Jesus encountered the Samaritan Woman at the well in John 4: 7-26, he told her, "If you knew the gift of God, and who it is that is saying to you, 'Give me a drink,' you would have asked him and he would have given you living water." Jesus went on to state further that everyone who drinks physical water will be thirsty again. This was in stark contrast to the spiritual water that he referenced that would become a spring of water in you welling up to eternal life.

When Christ left the earth and ascended into heaven, he did not leave us as orphans (John 14: 18). In contrast, God has predestined us for adoption to himself through Jesus Christ (Ephesians 1: 5) with an inheritance that is far greater than any our earthly fathers could give us. The Holy Spirit is available to those who belong to Christ as our helper, comforter and constant companion to equip us daily for all that lies ahead.

Self-care is important to ensure that you continue to operate smoothly and efficiently. However, there is no greater self-care than deliberately carving out personal time in your day to commune with the Spirit of God by feasting on the Word of God, praying to the Father and being still in his presence. By practically prioritizing time with God on a daily basis, He will fill your cup to overflowing so that others; your spouse, children, friends etc., can feast at your table without depleting your storehouse.

COUPLE ENRICHMENT EXERCISE

Enter your secret space with your spouse for Part A of this exercise.

Part A

- Download a free audio version of the Bible from YouTube.Com. The King James Dramatized Audio Bible is a great choice.
- Listen to the Psalms for 15 minutes starting at the beginning of the book.

- As you listen, lay side by side with your eyes closed.
- Take deep breaths, as you hold each other's hands and allow the Spirit of God to refresh you through the Word of God.

PART B

- After 15 minutes of listening take turns expressing to each other ways in which you both could start to prioritize self-care (i.e., activities that help you to unwind and reduce stress levels). For example, a nice warm bath together, listening to your favorite songs, a walk to the park, a candle light dinner and so on.
- Create a list of all the activities generated and post it on your bathroom mirror or another area that you visit frequently.
- Finally, schedule one day each week to do an activity on your list together.

PRAYER

Father, we are empty before You today and we need to be filled by You. Fill us with Your living water and grant us Your peace. Lord, we need You to grow. Help us to manage our time in order to prioritize being in Your presence, and teach us to care for ourselves and our marriage in practical ways. Father, You are the living water that refreshes, renews and revives us each day. Father, we ask You today to take complete control and to saturate us in

Your presence. Holy Spirit, comfort us, help us and motivate us to desire You more and more so that through God, our marriage will realize its full potential. In Jesus' name, we pray. Amen.

Day 10

What Do I Bring to The Table?

1 CORINTHIANS 13

1 If I speak in the tongues of men and of angels, but have
not love, I am a noisy gong or a clanging cymbal. 2 And if I
have prophetic powers, and understand all mysteries and all
knowledge, and if I have all faith, so as to remove
mountains, but have not love, I am nothing. 3 If I give
away all I have, and if I deliver up my body to be burned,
but have not love, I gain nothing.

4 Love is patient and kind; love does not envy or boast; it is
not arrogant 5 or rude. It does not insist on its own way; it
is not irritable or resentful; 6 it does not rejoice at
wrongdoing, but rejoices with the truth. 7 Love bears all
things, believes all things, hopes all things, endures all
things.

8 Love never ends. As for prophecies, they will pass away;
as for tongues, they will cease; as for knowledge, it will
pass away. 9 For we know in part and we prophesy in part,
10 but when the perfect comes, the partial will pass away.
11 When I was a child, I spoke like a child, I thought like a
child, I reasoned like a child. When I became a man, I gave

up childish ways. 12 For now we see in a mirror dimly, but then face to face. Now I know in part; then I shall know fully, even as I have been fully known.

13 So now faith, hope, and love abide, these three; but the greatest of these is love.

REFLECTION

Self-examination is never easy and yet it is a necessary habit to cultivate. Most partners are able to generate a laundry list of all the wonderful attributes they personally possess in order to present solid evidence in support of the case for, "I am the best thing that ever happened to you!" We belittle our partner's contributions to our lives and family, while consistently reminding them of what we bring to the table.

So there is no better time than the present to really take an inventory of what we really bring to the table. Before doing so, please revisit the Reflection on Day 6 concerning your decision to follow Christ's example. With all the amazing things that you have done, are doing and will do for your partner, are you like Christ? Do you love your wife? Do you respect your husband? Are you submitted one to another?

Jesus in Matthew 6: 1-6 cautions us to beware of practicing our righteousness to be seen by others. He further encourages us to give in secret expecting that as we do so our reward comes directly from God. Jesus' example of a marriage union also encourages us to aspire toward loving each other with such purity that our sole objective is each other's wellbeing. Adjusting your motive accordingly will allow you to delight in doing acts of love and kindness for your spouse without keeping a score sheet. Finally, by surrendering the right to consistently tell your partner what you are bringing to the table, you will henceforth refrain from violating the covenant you made with each other and with God.

COUPLE ENRICHMENT EXERCISE

Over the next week you will identify seven acts of kindness/love that you know is important to your spouse based on feedback they provided you in the past:

- For example, you know your wife has a deadline at work and is struggling to manage her usual responsibilities. Without making an announcement; clean the kitchen, put away the dishes then make sandwiches for dinner.
- Another example might be, relieving your husband of his responsibility to prepare the kids for bed simply because you noticed he was falling asleep when he arrived home.
- Be deliberate in ensuring that what you choose to do requires sacrifice on your part. In the preceding example, it would be fair to assume that you too were falling asleep, which means you were just as tired or even more tired than your husband.

- Do not allow yourself to expect a "thank you" for your efforts. Instead, pray and ask God to let his approval be enough for you.

PRAYER

Father, we submit ourselves to You and ask that You make us pliable so that we will learn from You. Today we depend on You to radiate Your agape love through us. Your divine love has the ability to soften our rough edges and prune us so that we express love that expects nothing in return. Teach us how to love each other as You have commanded. Allow us to mature in Christ and help us to work on our weaknesses and shortcomings that cause us to complain, hold a grudge, and hold on to feelings of bitterness, envy, and pride. Grant us a love that will go beyond our feelings by manifesting itself in practical acts that build each other, and sustain our marriage. Father, cultivate a spirit of meekness within us that reflects Your grace. Let our light so shine that others will see Christ in us. In Jesus' name, we pray. Amen.

Day 11

I Need You

PSALM 147: 3

He heals the brokenhearted and binds up their wounds.

REFLECTION

"I need you". These are three small words that are simple enough to say. Yet, do you ever take an honest look at your life and consider the degree to which you actually need your wife? Do you ever stop to consider what your day might look like if your husband were not a part of your life? We tend to focus on the big picture while neglecting the smaller details that collectively give form to the big picture. Or, in contrast, we tend to focus on the details and neglect to consider the big picture. Taking either of these extreme positions is typical in marriages. That is, you may focus on the little things your partner does not do well such as picking up after himself, but miss the fact that he has been reliable and consistent throughout the course of your relationship. Or you may focus on the perception that your partner is not as ambitious as you would like, but miss the fact that he makes himself available to care for the kids and the household chores which affords you the opportunities you have to pursue your dreams.

Many couples court divorce because they naively fantasize about how simple their lives will become once they are no longer shackled to a partner who adds little or no value. Yet divorce rarely offers the freedom and relief that most people anticipate it will. Additionally, one would be surprised at the number of partners who discover following the dissolution of their marriage that 1. They did, in fact, need their partner and 2. They are still not equipped to have a successful marriage to a new partner because they did not address their personal issues after their divorce.

To have a successful, satisfying and harmonious marriage, requires a deliberate shift in perspective. That is, you must develop the flexibility necessary to integrate the macro and micro perspectives in your life that allow you to recognize your need for and dependence on each other. Let's consider some reasons why you may not recognize the extent to which you do in fact need your partner: Your needs are far beyond your wife's human capacity to fulfill and your expectations of your husband to make you happy are unreasonable. This may not make sense to you. After all, why did I marry him if he could not make me happy? Isn't my wife supposed to fulfill my needs? The simplest answer to these questions is no.

The marriage union functions at its best when two people who are whole come together and because they are personally happy and content they are in a position to give and as such add value to each other's life. In contrast, when one (or both) partner has baggage, this partner is operating below capacity, thus placing undue pressure on their spouse to fill the void that exists in their heart.

The Reflection on Day 9 provided insight concerning who is responsible for filling your cup and causing it to overflow. As you come to recognize your ultimate dependence on God and become more deliberate in seeking his face, over time you will grow more content personally and as such begin to see your partner with greater clarity, appreciation, and compassion.

COUPLE ENRICHMENT EXERCISE

Today's task requires you to sit in silence with God and simply listen for 5 minutes. Use a timer. After five minutes have elapsed you will create a list of your unmet needs and desires. Aim to place a minimum of 10 items on your list.

- Before you begin writing, ask yourself these questions: What is missing from my life? What makes me happy? What makes me unhappy?
- After formulating a picture in your mind concerning the questions asked, begin to list those things that you believe would make you happy.
- Having done so, divide your list into two categories: My Wife/Husband's Responsibility and My Responsibility

- Having completed your list, review it carefully then make a second list with the following heading: God's Responsibility.
- Finally, add items from your first list to the second, but only if you are prepared to trust God to work out and satisfy these needs on your behalf.

PRAYER

Father, You are our source and You are more than enough for us. Help us to recognize that our hope, joy and our peace come from You. Help us to come to terms with the void in our hearts that signify a need that is satisfied only by You. We need You, Lord. We need You to satisfy our unmet needs and we need You to be the center of our marriage and the wellspring of living water from which we draw our sustenance. Father, give us reasonable expectations of each other so that we do not place undue stress on our marriage. Father, we need You to help us to trust You completely as You mold and perfect us. Father, we acknowledge that we are complete in You and therefore, we have the potential to have a loving and fulfilling relationship with each other. In Jesus' name, we pray. Amen.

Day 12

I Love You, But...

THE SONG OF SOLOMON 1: 15-16

15 Behold, you are beautiful, my love; behold, you are beautiful; your eyes are doves. 16 Behold, you are beautiful, my beloved, truly delightful.

REFLECTION

Do you love your wife? Do you love your husband? "Yes, but I'm not in love..." This is one of the most common responses that partners give when asked if they love their spouse. We make this distinction between loving our spouse and being in-love with them without understanding the difference and the implications. The two experiences can usually be distinguished as follows: Love is a choice. It is deliberate, conscious and effortful, but is generally more enduring. Being in-love, in contrast, is primarily an emotional experience. It appears to happen effortlessly, is self-reinforcing and is more personally rewarding.

Typically the trajectory of marriage is that the in-love phase is dominant in the beginning, but tapers off as the couple settles into a routine. A shift from being in love with each other to loving each other gradually occurs at this phase. However, couples who understand the nature of relationship cycles are in a position to use this knowledge to harness their relationship, reignite passion and to fall in love with each other again. In contrast, transition phases are far more challenging for couples who do not understand relationship cycles. Furthermore, couples who fail to actively invest in their marriage could progress to a state of alienation that causes them to contemplate separation or divorce.

Consider two couple experiences that will add further clarity. Couple A is deeply passionate and in-love with each other when they marry. They continue to experience these emotions during the first year of their marriage, but notice that the intensity is decreasing. This concerns them deeply and causes them to worry that they are falling out of love with each other. They respond by complaining to friends and others who are equally inexperienced who inadvertently reinforce their fears. Couple B has a similar beginning but, upon noticing that the intensity of their emotions was decreasing, responded by prioritizing their marriage and making deliberate efforts to nurture their relationship.

Many couples enter marriage with unrealistic expectations and are unprepared to face the reality of marriage. The reality of marriage is that the in-love phase is less enduring than the love-phase. With that said, when couples understand that a marriage will not thrive in the absence of deliberate efforts to invest time and energy into each other, only then will they come to realize and appreciate that they will have the opportunity to fall in-love with each other many times over the course of their marriage. Alternately, couples who persistently fail to consistently nurture their marriage inevitably grow apart and become alienated from each other. These couples are more likely to experience what may be incorrectly perceived as irreconcilable differences leading to separation and/or divorce.

COUPLE ENRICHMENT EXERCISE

Your emotions are influenced by your thoughts and also by your actions. The exercise today is a behavioral experiment.

Husbands:

- Over the next three days, practice chivalry. Consistently open doors for your wife. Compliment her appearance, provide hugs spontaneously and use names of endearment each time you address her.

Wives:

- Initiate activities your husband enjoys, even if you disapprove. Watch a basketball or soccer game with him depending on what he likes. Play his favorite video game with him. Text him something that is meant for his eyes only especially if you plan to follow-up later… and you should.

As you engage in this exercise, observe the types of thoughts that filter through your mind. Pay careful attention to the ratio of positive to negative thoughts. As well, pay attention to the feelings that you are experiencing over the three days and the associated shift that occurs in your perception of the relationship.

PRAYER

Father, we need You more than ever. We desire to have the experience of falling in love with each other. Therefore, we ask You to give us the will to do the things that will cause us to experience the satisfaction associated with the feeling of being in love. Father, motivate us to invest the time, available resources and energy to improve our relationship. We desire to enjoy each other, to be each other's best friend and life partner, and to form an enduring bond that is not easily broken. We re-commit ourselves to You and to each other and ask that You help us to appreciate and love each other even when we find it difficult to do so. Father, remove the "But" from our love by giving us the capacity to love each other unconditionally. In Jesus' name, we pray, Amen.

Day 13

The Way It Used to Be

ISAIAH 54: 17

"No weapon that is fashioned against you shall succeed, and you shall refute every tongue that rises against you in judgment. This is the heritage of the servants of the LORD and their vindication from me, declares the LORD."

REFLECTION

It is easy for couples to feel a sense of despair as they look back at the early years of their marriage and become stuck on, "the way it used to be". They often lament that their partner has changed especially as they become increasingly critical of a spouse they now perceive as distant and unloving.

When couples get caught in this riptide it becomes extremely difficult for them to rise above it as their behaviors toward each other constitute a self-reinforcing cycle that begins to define the relationship: She complains and he withdraws pushing her to complain some more. Although couples tend to resort to complaining as their primary line of defense they do not immediately recognize that God is concerned with the smallest of details of their relationship and is an ever present help in their time of need. Turning to God to seek his guidance in navigating these challenging phases of your marriage will accomplish much more than your "complain-withdraw" solution to problems.

With God fighting for your marriage, there is no weapon formed against you that will prosper. Therefore, the way it used to be is helpful only if you allow God to use it to inspire you, and to motivate you to work on having a relationship that is more consistent with the potential He ordained for your marriage.

COUPLE ENRICHMENT EXERCISE

I would like you, for a brief moment, to imagine that you have been seeking God concerning your marriage and without warning, he answers your prayer and grants you a miracle: That is, you have the Best Marriage Possible.

Now let's take a solution-focused orientation to your marriage. Use a recording device to record your conversation as you take turns expressing the following:

- Tell your partner, using specific examples, how she is acting differently towards you now that God has granted you a miracle. In other words, what are the clues that allow you to recognize that God has granted you this miracle?
- For example, you may say something like: "I come home and you stop what you are doing for 10

minutes to give me a hug and a kiss and to sit beside me briefly before resuming your tasks".

- Do not stop there. Talk about what happens in the mornings when you wake up.
- What happens when you are visiting relatives and friends?
- What happens when you are lying in bed before falling asleep?
- Keep going until you have a clear picture of your ideal marriage.

PRAYER

Father, we desire to grow and to make changes that would enhance our marriage. We pray that You will take our efforts and bless them so that we will see Your glory manifested in our marriage. Enable us to use the memories of our past to motivate us to respect and love each other and help us to use our challenges as a catalyst to build character. In Jesus' name, we pray. Amen.

"When couples get caught in this riptide it becomes extremely difficult for them to rise above it as their behaviors toward each other constitute a self-reinforcing cycle that begins to define the relationship: She complains and he withdraws pushing her to complain some more." p. 67

Day 14

I Want to Be the Best...

1 PETER 3: 1-9

1 In the same way, you wives, be submissive to your own
husbands so that even if any of them are disobedient to the
word, they may be won without a word by the behavior of
their wives, 2 as they observe your chaste and respectful
behavior. 3 Your adornment must not be merely external—
braiding the hair, and wearing gold jewelry, or putting on
dresses; 4 but let it be the hidden person of the heart, with
the imperishable quality of a gentle and quiet spirit, which
is precious in the sight of God. 5 For in this way in former
times the holy women also, who hoped in God, used to
adorn themselves, being submissive to their own husbands;
6 just as Sarah obeyed Abraham, calling him lord, and you
have become her children if you do what is right without
being frightened by any fear.

7 You husbands in the same way, live with your wives in
an understanding way, as with someone weaker, since she
is a woman; and show her honor as a fellow heir of the
grace of life, so that your prayers will not be hindered.
8 To sum up, all of you be harmonious, sympathetic,
brotherly, kind-hearted, and humble in spirit; 9 not
returning evil for evil or insult for insult, but giving a

blessing instead; for you were called for the very purpose that you might inherit a blessing.

REFLECTION

Every married couple should desire to have the best marriage. Consistent with this desire each partner should want to be the best husband/ best wife possible. Being the best wife does not happen when your husband is worthy. Likewise, being the best husband is not contingent on having a wife that is good enough.

Let's consider in parallel the life of Daniel, who purposed in his heart not to defile himself with the king's delicacies although he was living in conditions where it would be far easier to conform to what was expected. Daniel wasn't married but stay with this train of thought for a moment. You are living in a society that teaches that one hand scratches the other and unless a relationship is reciprocal you should walk away and seek greener pastures. After all, you deserve better than your spouse is giving you.

The latter is likely true, but if you like Daniel were to take a stand that my commitment to God supersedes my circumstances you would come to recognize that your marriage is a covenant relationship with God. Honoring this covenant requires you to purpose in your heart to be the best husband and to be the best wife you can be in spite of your circumstances. The outcome of Daniel's stance was God's favour throughout his time in Babylon. Likewise, you can expect that as you honor God through your commitment to your spouse, he will reward you accordingly. Furthermore, you are more likely to effect change in your spouse by changing yourself.

COUPLE ENRICHMENT EXERCISE

Mentorship and accountability are indispensable ingredients for your personal growth and development as a couple. Discuss the following with each other:

- Which couples do we know that we believe are potentially suitable role-models of a Christ-centered marriage?
- Create a short list of the couples identified then pray concerning the couple that God desires to use to mentor you as you work on having a great marriage.
- Schedule a meeting with the couple selected, share your 30-Day journey with them then ask if they would prayerfully consider entering into a Covenant-Accountability Relationship with you.
- This covenant would involve meeting approximately once every three months to check in with you, pray and fellowship together, and to share your successes and challenges.

PRAYER

Father, we come before You today because we know that You gave Your best for us when You sacrificed Your Son, Jesus Christ. Father, we are able to approach You with everything that concerns us because of that sacrifice. Lord, it is extremely difficult to demonstrate love consistently, especially in an atmosphere where we are deeply hurt and offended. Therefore, we intentionally give ourselves to You to transform us into the husband and wife that You have ordained. Help us to encourage each other and to reflect Christ's character traits in our actions and attitudes so that we can experience Your continued favour in our lives. In Jesus' name, we pray. Amen.

Day 15

How Do I Enhance Your Life?

MATTHEW 6: 1-4

1 “Beware of practicing your righteousness before other
people in order to be seen by them, for then you will have
no reward from your Father who is in heaven. 2 “Thus,
when you give to the needy, sound no trumpet before you,
as the hypocrites do in the synagogues and in the streets,
that they may be praised by others. Truly, I say to you, they
have received their reward. 3 But when you give to the
needy, do not let your left hand know what your right hand
is doing, 4 so that your giving may be in secret. And your
Father who sees in secret will reward you.

REFLECTION

Imagine what your marriage would be like if you each focus your effort on doing things that enhance each other’s life. This is the recipe for a great marriage. Think about it this way. There would be no need to worry about whether your partner would reciprocate and/or take your efforts for granted because you would each be committed to prioritizing each other’s well-being.

You are being challenged today to give consideration to the feedback you have been given by your partner over the duration of your relationship. What has your wife consistently complained about? What has your husband repeatedly requested of you either directly or indirectly? For today, let go of the fact that there is so much that you desire from your partner that is not forthcoming and consider the words of Jesus who teaches us that it is better to give than to receive. As you do so, however, if this seems too difficult to do consistently, bring to remembrance what was said earlier, "Imagine what your marriage would look like if you each focus your effort on doing things that enhance each other's life." Not only that, but you have an opportunity to covenant with God with the assurance that as you obediently give selflessly to your spouse your reward of a healthy, secure and mutually satisfying relationship comes directly from God.

COUPLE ENRICHMENT EXERCISE

There are many things that you require of each other. The Reflection on Day 10 (What Do I Bring to the Table?) challenged you to do specific acts of kindness and love that you were not expected to seek recognition for. Today you get to take turns sharing your honest reaction to the experiment with each other.

- What was it like to make sacrifices for your spouse without directly letting them know?
- What was it like to make sacrifices for your spouse without receiving validation for doing so?

- What were the benefits of the exercise?
- What were the challenges encountered during the exercise?

PRAYER

Father, we come together for You to show us the opportunities we have to enhance each other's life. We both desire to have a harmonious and healthy relationship. Therefore, show us the gaps in our marriage and fill us with Your grace as we partner with You and with each other in learning how to give selflessly. We further ask that You give us a new perspective on our marriage, "to see that it is better to give than to receive". In Jesus' name, we pray. Amen.

"This is the recipe for a great marriage. Think about it this way. There would be no need to worry about whether your partner would reciprocate and/or take your efforts for granted because you would each be committed to prioritizing each other's well-being." p. 75

Day 16

Could We Give This a Try?

JAMES 2: 14-26

14 What good is it, my brothers, if someone says he has faith but does not have works? Can that faith save him? 15 If a brother or sister is poorly clothed and lacking in daily food, 16 and one of you says to them, "Go in peace, be warmed and filled," without giving them the things needed for the body, what good is that? 17 So also faith by itself, if it does not have works, is dead.

18 But someone will say, "You have faith and I have works." Show me your faith apart from your works, and I will show you my faith by my works. 19 You believe that God is one; you do well. Even the demons believe—and shudder! 20 Do you want to be shown, you foolish person, that faith apart from works is useless? 21 Was not Abraham our father justified by works when he offered up his son Isaac on the altar? 22 You see that faith was active along with his works, and faith was completed by his works; 23 and the Scripture was fulfilled that says, "Abraham believed God, and it was counted to him as righteousness"—and he was called a friend of God. 24 You

see that a person is justified by works and not by faith alone. 25 And in the same way was not also Rahab the prostitute justified by works when she received the messengers and sent them out by another way? 26 For as the body apart from the spirit is dead, so also faith apart from works is dead.

REFLECTION

Relationships are not static and yet we often act as though they are. Your marriage has become stale over time… and why wouldn't it? You do the same things over and over. Wake up, bathe, eat, fuss over your kids (or pets), peck on the cheek (if you are fortunate), go to work, come home, eat, fuss over your kids some more, make love (if you are really really fortunate and maybe it's Christmas or Monday night). Okay, I'm pushing the limits a bit, but let's face it when was the last time you tried something new.

Sit on your husband's lap even if you worry that he may want to go further. Prepare a meal together that you both have not had in years. Go to the community center for skating. Learn the waltz and try to avoid stepping on each other's toes because if you do you'll have too much to laugh about tonight and run the risk of being late for work tomorrow. Go for a walk together. Husband's, if physically possible (and this is not a dare), allow your wife to climb on your back just for fun. Have a pillow fight and make sure you use a feather pillow so that it will make a memorable mess. Chase each other like teenagers with a bucket of water and ice. Have a camp night on your living room floor…

Do not protest that you are too busy. What is your priority? God will make a way for you to have the best marriage possible that is commensurate with the desires of your heart. Stated differently, your efforts become the necessary "works" that must accompany your faith.

COUPLE ENRICHMENT EXERCISE

Review the list of activities mentioned in the reflection section then:

- Make arrangements for the upcoming weekend to do one new activity that takes you outside of your comfort zone each week.

PRAYER

Father, please give us the flexibility we need to break away from the routine ways in which we interact with each other that causes us to stagnate in our marriage. We desire to incorporate spontaneous, and fun activities into our daily experiences that stimulate intimacy and excitement. Father, we ask You to renew our minds. Take away our inhibitions with each other and teach us to make deliberate efforts to use our faith with works to add flavour and to infuse passion. In Jesus' name, we pray. Amen.

"Relationships are not static and yet we often act as though they are. Your marriage has become stale over time… and why wouldn't it? You do the same things over and over. Wake up, bathe, eat, fuss over your kids (or pets), peck on the cheek (if you are fortunate), go to work, come home, eat, fuss over your kids some more, make love (if you are really really fortunate and maybe it's Christmas or Monday night). Okay, I'm pushing the limits a bit, but let's face it when was the last time you tried something new." p. 80

Day 17

Instead of Talking, Could We Do…?

PROVERBS 25:24

24 It is better to live in a corner of the housetop than in a house shared with a quarrelsome wife.

REFLECTION

I'm going to make a sweeping generalization about relationship dynamics. Most men do not like to talk about their relationship with their wives. I have no statistics on hand, but I'm fairly confident that this assertion is correct. Do you like it when your wife approaches you and says, "We need to talk?" If you look forward to those moments, I commend you sincerely. However, you are the exception. I've raised this issue because it is perhaps one of the biggest challenges that couples struggle with to no avail. Women tend to want to solve problems by "talking", whereas men have a distinct preference for "doing". To complicate matters further, both tend to be equally committed to the infallibility of their position and could not imagine why the other would even think to say/do otherwise. Aw marriage (sigh).

Well, I consider myself a fair person and even though I am a wife I have no choice but to bat for both teams. In other words, I'm playing for both Team Wives and Team Husbands. To ensure there is no misunderstanding, let me state for the record that, "You are both right and you are both wrong". Talking with each other regularly is necessary to solve problems, learn about each other, cultivate intimacy and the list is in-exhaustive. But… wives before you begin to celebrate the home-run I just scored for Team Wives, please continue reading to the end.

Criticizing your husband, complaining, saying the same thing over and over, otherwise known as "nagging", is not problem-solving. In fact, it is unreasonable to keep saying the same thing repeatedly and yet expect a different result. Wisdom would dictate that if you want a different result, perhaps it's time to try a different approach. Do things with your husband. Support him in his efforts to fix the problems and validate his efforts by showing your appreciation regularly.

This will be challenging for you and may not feel authentic but do not give up prematurely. Instead, first try talking to your Heavenly Father to gain greater clarity on issues and to vent your frustrations. You will be pleasantly surprised to learn that God is not far removed from your circumstances, and He does respond in very tangible ways. Afterwards, you are encouraged to approach your husband with specific suggestions to solve the problem. For example, rather than complain that he is inconsiderate… try suggesting that he keeps the kids for two hours on a Saturday between 12:00-2:00 pm so that you can get your nails done or otherwise engage in well-deserved self-care activities. You will both have a greater opportunity to succeed at solving relationship problems when you try this approach.

COUPLE ENRICHMENT EXERCISE

Husbands:

- Turn off the TV, cell phones and computers for 15 minutes daily and just allow your wives to have your undivided attention for conversation.

Wives:

- Practice letting go of the need to talk about the problem and instead; ask your husband what he thinks you should do about it; then allow him to try to fix it when he offers to do so.

PRAYER

Father, teach us alternative ways to communicate with each other in order to be sensitive to our differences, and to be more effective at solving problems. We often become judgmental and defensive as we relate to each other. Therefore, take away the spirit of pride that causes us to complain about, and criticize each other. Teach us to use creative solutions to our problems that improve our relationship and grant us patience to support each other as we surrender control of our marriage to you. In Jesus' name, we pray. Amen.

Day 18

What's in Your Heart?

PROVERBS 25: 14
A word fitly spoken is like apples of gold in a setting of silver.

REFLECTION
Today's reflection is a continuation of Day 17 - Reflection (Instead of Talking, could we do…?). Husbands, you will not connect with your wives if you refuse to talk with them. Couples who do not communicate well will struggle to bond with each other. Wives, it may come as a surprise to you, but your husbands probably have a lot more to say than you realize. The likely reason is that women tend to take the lead in conversations with their husbands. Additionally, having taken the lead, they also assume responsibility for selecting the topic and setting the pace for the conversation that ensues. To be fair to you, no one would blame you for doing so. Besides, there is a legitimate fear that if you don't you'd probably have no relationship with him because he does not initiate conversation with you. Nonetheless, I would like to present you with an alternate perspective.

Being a leader in this area of your marriage can work to your advantage if you learn how to humbly lead from behind. When your desire is to really know what's in your spouse's heart you will take initiative to expand your repertoire of interests. Yes, show interest in the things your husband is interested in. Follow the stock market, so you will have more than, "you are distant and unavailable" to talk about. You say he is acting like a big kid when he plays his video games. Yet, what do you have to lose by having a conversation with your husband that sounds more like, "You are really good at this game. What's your top score?" instead of, "You are wasting time on this game! You don't spend enough time with your family".

When you begin to show interest with no motive beyond simply understanding what's dear to your partner's heart, you will find that conversations in your marriage begin to flow more organically. They become less punishing for your partner and the underlining feeling of dread that usually accompanies the, "we need to talk" startup will give way to an atmosphere of mutual interest and openness.

Wives, just in case you are feeling fearful that your issues and concerns will never be addressed, I would like to reassure you that it is far more productive to have a conversation with a partner that is not defensive. Spending the time nurturing your relationship in this manner will allow you to reap considerable benefits. Oh, and one more thing, you will also begin to find that you have far less to complain about on a daily basis because the obvious issues that bother you are probably symptoms of your underlining need for emotional closeness and intimacy with your husband.

COUPLE ENRICHMENT EXERCISE

Get ready to do some Investigative research. Plan a date night where you go out together for a meal. This allows you to talk. Wives interview your husbands during your date by asking the following questions:

- What is your favorite activity to do with your male friends?
- What is your favorite sport?
- What is your favorite TV program?
- What is your favorite car?
- What is your favorite magazine?

As you read the list provided keep in mind that every male is different. The above is merely an example to give you a starting place for your interview. After completing your interview, you will do some personal research to learn more about your husband's interests so that you can converse with him from an informed perspective.

PRAYER

Father, we come before You today because You know our hearts and the intentions of our minds. Show us how to relate to each other's interests. Teach us how to assume a supportive role in relation to each other's interests. Father, help us to nurture each in a manner that evokes positive emotions as well as stimulates closeness. In Jesus' name, we pray. Amen.

Day 19

Do You Like it When I...?

PHILIPPIANS 4:9

What you have learned and received and heard and seen in me – practice these things, and the God of peace will be with you.

REFLECTION

Many people get more out of the process of venting than they do from solving problems. Resultantly, they fail to achieve the goals that they would like to accomplish in their marriage. Let's aim to create a fundamental shift in the way you handle the things you perceive as problems. Let's begin to treat the problems as opportunities for growth and personal development.

Mentorship, as was noted in Day14 - Reflection (I Want to Be the Best...), is an important aspect of success in marriage. You can learn a great deal from observing others who are effective at the things you struggle with in order to practise these behaviours in your marriage. Marriage is a learning curve and you don't get to have a great marriage without experimenting with new behaviours. When you experiment with new behaviours you will get more from the experience by incorporating a feedback process that helps you determine how your spouse is being impacted by the changes.

COUPLE ENRICHMENT EXERCISE

Once more, observe other Christian couples you have a relationship with and note the behaviours you believe they are effective at demonstrating. No couple is perfect, so keep your expectations reasonable and remember that you learn from positive as well as negative examples. As you observe, ask yourself questions like the following:

- Do you like the way that she speaks to her husband in a gentle voice although it is obvious she does not agree with his assertion?
- Do you like the way that he typically opens doors for his wife?
- Do you like the way he says, I can't give you a response at this moment, I would like some time to talk it over with my wife first?
- Do you like the way she hugs her husband and says, take all the time you need to work through it. I'm right here when you need me.

Try to implement some of these behaviors in your marriage, then later solicit feedback from your partner. Your feedback process should resemble the following examples:

- "Do you like it when I ask you about your day?"

- "Do you like it when I hold your hand when we are out with our friends?"
- What did you like about it?

Be open to your partner's feedback. As well, be mindful of each other's efforts and aim to reward rather than punish those efforts. Finally, keep in mind that if you dismiss or ignore those efforts the likelihood of your partner persisting with their new behaviour decreases.

PRAYER

Father, we ask You today to help us to be open with each other. There are times when we do not know how to behave appropriately in private and in public. At those times we allow our emotions to get the best of us and often behave in dishonorable ways. Show us examples of acceptable behaviors in other couples with whom we interact and motivate us to practice what we observe. Father, we ask You today to give us self-control as we interact with each other and aim to resolve the concerns we have. In Jesus' name, we pray. Amen.

“Many people get more out of the process of venting than they do from solving problems. Resultantly, they fail to achieve the goals that they would like to accomplish in their marriage.” p. 91

Day 20

On a Scale of 1 – 10, How Satisfied are You?

1 CORINTHIANS 7:5 (AMP)

5 Do not deprive each other [of marital rights], except perhaps by mutual consent for a time, so that you may devote yourselves [unhindered] to prayer, but come together again so that Satan will not tempt you [to sin] because of your lack of self-control.

REFLECTION

Today is a big day. Today you both get to ask an important question. How satisfied are you with your sex life? Oh, come on… you can't pick up a book on marriage and not address sexual intimacy. Do you talk to each other about your needs and desires? If you don't, how can you be sure you are both satisfied? The marriage bed must be kept undefiled (Hebrews 13:4). Ensuring that your marriage is held in honor will take deliberate efforts on both your part to ensure that neither of you is left vulnerable to temptations including sexual immorality and adultery.

Many married couples struggle with sexual intimacy. The reasons vary but fall under the general categories of; physiological, emotional and psychological factors that manifest themselves in problems related to performance, desire, pain and so on. It may come as a surprise to many Christian couples that the God who created the universe also created sexual intercourse, made it pure and beautiful to be enjoyed within the matrimonial bed and as such is available in their time of struggle. Therefore, today is an opportunity for you to begin to prioritize this aspect of your marriage by learning how to talk with each other more openly and how to seek God for greater connection and deeper levels of intimacy with each other.

COUPLE ENRICHMENT EXERCISE

Let's Talk About Our Sex Life Worksheet

"Couples should develop the art of sincerely and openly discussing their sexual fantasies and needs… Learning to speak openly with your partner about your needs, likes, and dislikes will improve the overall health of your relationship" (Townsend, 2013).

Please answer the following questions as openly as you can:

1. When do you feel most connected to your partner?

____

____

____

____

____

____

____

2. Rate your current perception of your level of intimacy on a scale of 0 to 10 (0 – No connection; 10 – Amazing!).

0---1---2---3---4---5---6---7---8---9---10

3. What is your definition of Great Sex?

____

____

____

____

____

____

____

4. Use one word/ phrase to describe sex with your husband/wife.

____

____

____

____

____

5. Rate your current level of sexual satisfaction experienced with your partner on a scale of 0 to 10 (0 – Very Dissatisfied; 10 – 100% Satisfied!).

0---1---2---3---4---5---6---7---8---9---10

6. After reading this book, you go to bed later tonight and a miracle happens. The miracle is that you have achieved the level of intimate connection you've yearned for with your partner and your sex life is exactly as you had imagined it would be. Describe in detail, what is happening between you and your partner now that there has been a "miracle"!

Wives

____
____
____
____
____
____
____
____

Husband

____
____
____
____
____
____
____
____

Worksheet Created by Ghia Townsend (May 23, 2013).

PRAYER

Father, teach us to be open with You in every area of our marriage. We will not hide our nakedness from You as Adam and Eve did after they sinned against You. We ask that You enable us to enjoy the gift You have created for our pleasure. Enable us to overcome our inhibitions with each other and motivate us to be proactive in the bedroom.

Teach us to be more playful with each other and ignite excitement within us so that we will no longer experience a sense of boredom. Awaken our desires and passion for each other. Father, we pray that our expressions of love will honour You as we strive to keep our matrimonial bed undefiled. In Jesus' name, we pray. Amen.

Day 21

What Could I Do to Improve?

GENESIS 2: 24-25

24 Therefore a man shall leave his father and his mother and hold fast to his wife, and they shall become one flesh.
25 And the man and his wife were both naked and were not ashamed.

REFLECTION

To grow we need to risk feeling vulnerable with our spouse. In fact, what is more vulnerable than being in-love with someone? We feel like we need them all the time and that opens us up to the possibility that we could experience hurt and or rejection in spite of their best intentions. It is better to risk being vulnerable to your spouse, although you recognize they could hurt you, than to be guarded with them. Feeling vulnerable is an unavoidable part of the process if you desire a closer bond with your spouse. In contrast, if you chose to remain guarded and heavily defended, you will not grow personally and especially as a couple.

COUPLE ENRICHMENT EXERCISE

Get into the habit of inviting constructive feedback from your spouse. For today's assignment you will engage in the following discussion related to your responses on the "Let's Talk About Our Sex-life" Worksheet. Ask your partner the following questions based on their actual responses:

- "Hon, you rated our level of intimacy as a 3. What could I do differently that would cause you to improve this rating?"
- "Hon, you rated your level of satisfaction with our sex life as a 5. What could I change that would cause you to improve that rating?"

As a side note, when the potential is high for you to become defensive with each other try the following:

- Deliberately lower your voice or soften your tone
- Use a name of endearment (e.g., Baby, Babes Lovie, Dear, Sweet Heart/ Sweets/ Sweetie or Sugar Dumpling – if you are Jamaican)
- Refrain from holding your breath
- And don't forget to touch your partner gently as you speak.

I won't get technical by using psychological jargons to explain why this works. I'll simply ask you to try these techniques then encourage you to observe, for yourself what happens to your heart rate, pulse for example. You will discover that by following these simple suggestions, you are able to keep your emotions well-regulated so you could have an engaging and productive conversation.

PRAYER

Father, we place ourselves before You and ask that You shape us as we aspire to improve the way we relate to each other. Teach us how to humble ourselves so that we will be receptive to each other's feedback. Help us to not feel offended when the feedback provided is inconsistent with our expectations. We ask You to give us understanding and clarity as we share our honest assessments with each other. Father, we desire to be flexible and adaptable. Therefore, please help us to adjust our behaviors so that we will learn how to please You as we aim to please each other. In Jesus' name, we pray. Amen.

"Get into the habit of inviting constructive feedback from your spouse. For today's assignment you will engage in the following discussion related to your responses on the "Let's Talk About Our Sex-life" Worksheet." p. 102

Day 22

Could We Try That Today?

PROVERBS 6:4-11 (NLT)

4 Don’t put it off; do it now! Don’t rest until you do. 5 Save
yourself like a gazelle escaping from a hunter, like a bird
fleeing from a net. 6 Take a lesson from the ants, you
lazybones. Learn from their ways and become wise!
7 Though they have no prince or governor or ruler to make
them work, 8 they labor hard all summer, gathering food for
the winter. 9 But you, lazybones, how long will you sleep?
When will you wake up? 10 A little extra sleep, a little more
slumber, a little folding of the hands to rest— 11 then
poverty will pounce on you like a bandit; scarcity will
attack you like an armed robber.

REFLECTION

Now things are really getting interesting. Days 20 through 21 are related. Things will not improve if all you do is talk about them. You must do them. You have given your wife invaluable feedback concerning what she could do differently that would cause you to feel more satisfied sexually: “Darling, I would like it if you initiated sex occasionally. That would make me feel like you are just as attracted to me as I am to you.” Likewise, you have identified and shared a few specific things that your husband could do or say that would cause you to feel more intimate and as such increase the rating you provided: "Sweetheart, I would like it if you came home and sat on the couch for 10-15 minutes and just hold me without any expectation that we will make love. I want you to ask me how I'm feeling and listen, really listen when I speak."

COUPLE ENRICHMENT EXERCISE

Why are you still reading? Go on, put the book away its time to try what you have discussed…

PRAYER

Father, we know we have been learning from You as we seek you concerning our marriage. Therefore, we ask You today to help us identify and attend to our specific needs. We also ask you to motivate and quicken us as we put what we have learned into practice today. In Jesus' name, we pray. Amen.

Day 23

What is Our Foundation?

MATTHEW 7: 24-27

[24] "Anyone who listens to my teaching and follows it is
wise, like a person who builds a house on solid
rock. [25] Though the rain comes in torrents and the
floodwaters rise and the winds beat against that house, it
won't collapse because it is built on bedrock. [26] But anyone
who hears my teaching and doesn't obey it is foolish, like a
person who builds a house on sand. [27] When the rains and
floods come and the winds beat against that house, it will
collapse with a mighty crash."

REFLECTION

Your husband is God's gift to you. Your wife is God's gift to you. Even so, a gift can be taken away from you. Job at the peak of his tribulation recognized that the Lord gives and he takes away (Job 1:21). It is not enough to be a Christian couple. The statistics concerning the failure rates of marriages, including Christian, marriages is staggering. Trials will come and you will be tested. When that happens, how will you fare? Will your marriage survive the storm? As for me and my house: We have survived one storm after another including; infidelity, sickness, financial hardships, and caring for a chronically ill child. We've weathered the storms not because I'm a professional Marriage Therapists, or because my husband and I are perfect, but by the grace of Jesus Christ who is the Lord of our house and our marriage. Christ is the Solid Rock on which we stand. He is our foundation.

John 16: 33 states, "I have said these things to you, that in me you may have peace. In the world you will have tribulation. But take heart; I have overcome the world." Your marriage will inevitably be tested beyond your capacity to overcome: An extramarital affair, a child outside of your matrimonial home, a challenging in-law, addictions, alienated affections, unforgiveness, selfishness, emotional, psychological and or physical abuse, separation or even divorce. The God who gave you this marriage is more than able to mend what is broken and to make it beautiful. Choose this day on which foundation you will build your marriage. Will you build it on the Solid Rock, where Christ is at the center? Or will you build it on the sand, where your commitment to each other is based on your emotions?

COUPLE ENRICHMENT EXERCISE

You will simply spend some time reflecting on what you read today. Give it due consideration then discuss with each other what you both believe is the foundation on which your marriage stands.

PRAYER

Father, You are our sure and solid foundation. In You, we move and have our being. You are our source of strength, security, and stability. Your grace is sufficient for us and we ask that You perfect Your power in our weaknesses. Father, forgive us for excluding You from our daily experiences. We acknowledge You today as our foundation and we place our trust in Christ alone. In Jesus' name, we pray. Amen.

"The statistics concerning the failure rates of marriages, including Christian marriages, is staggering. Trials will come and you will be tested. When that happens, how will you fare? Will your marriage survive the storm?" p. 107

Day 24

Lord, You are Our Refuge and Fortress

PSALM 71: 1-5

1 In you, O LORD, do I take refuge; let me never be put to shame! 2 In your righteousness deliver me and rescue me; incline your ear to me, and save me! 3 Be to me a rock of refuge, to which I may continually come; you have given the command to save me, for you are my rock and my fortress. 4 Rescue me, O my God, from the hand of the wicked, from the grasp of the unjust and cruel man. 5 For you, O Lord, are my hope, my trust, O LORD, from my youth.

REFLECTION

The Lord is your refuge and your fortress. He is with you always. He is available in your time of trouble and he will fight on your behalf as you continue to seek His face in faith. You are children of the living God and as such your inheritance is immense. Consider and claim the following promises for your marriage:

- No weapon that is fashioned against you shall succeed, and you shall refute every tongue that rises against you in judgment. This is the heritage / of the servants of the Lord and their vindication from me, declares the Lord. (Isaiah 54:17).

- And I am sure of this, that he who began a good work in you will bring it to completion at the day of Jesus Christ. (Philippians 1:6)
- For I know the plans I have for you, declares the LORD, plans for welfare and not for evil, to give you a future and a hope (Jeremiah 29:11)
- For as the rain and the snow come down from heaven and do not return there but water the earth, making it bring forth and sprout, giving seed to the sower and bread to the eater, so shall my word be that goes out from my mouth; it shall not return to me empty, but it shall accomplish that which I purpose, and shall succeed in the thing for which I sent it. For you shall go out in joy and be led forth in peace; the mountains and the hills before you shall break forth into singing, and all the trees of the field shall clap their hands (Isaiah 55: 10-12)

COUPLE ENRICHMENT EXERCISE

Rest in the assurance of these promises. Declare God's word over your marriage and repeat them often lest you should forget whose you really are.

PRAYER

Father, we take You at Your word and rely on Your promises today. You are our refuge and our strength. Hide us and give us Your peace in our time of trouble. You are high and lifted up! Yet You, Oh, Lord, reach down to us, reveal Yourself to us, and allow us to experience joy and hope. Teach us to depend solely on You and create in us a new heart. Today, we rejoice in You and we declare Your glory to the ends of the earth. Father, we surrender our will to You as You do a complete work in us. We are Yours forever. In Jesus' name, we pray. Amen.

"The Lord is your refuge and your fortress. He is with you always. He is available in your time of trouble and he will fight on your behalf as you continue to seek His face in faith." P. 111

Day 25

Lord, Be a Fence Around Us

ZACHARIAH 2: 5

And I will be to her a wall of fire all around, declares the LORD, and I will be the glory in her midst.

REFLECTION

We have heard the saying, "An apple a day keeps the doctor away". Likewise, the couple that prays together stays together. It is important that you begin to raise each other up in prayer. Get into the habit of holding each other and praying for each other. In the presence of your partner, ask God to bless their health, career, extended family and so on. Declare the Word of God over each other by speaking the things that aren't as though they were, "Father, thank you for giving me this husband who is kind, loving, compassionate, caring, accountable, reliable, honest, trustworthy" etc. "Thank you for my beautiful wife who sacrifices for her family daily despite feeling tired and overwhelmed by the daily demands on her time. Thank you for this beautiful woman who loves me unconditionally and who does her very best to support me in my interests, my career" etcetera.

You may object to saying these things reasoning that this would not be true. But, I am challenging you to declare these words by faith and see what the Lord does.

COUPLE ENRICHMENT EXERCISE

- Read Ezekiel 37: 1-6 together: 1 The hand of the LORD was upon me, and he brought me out in the Spirit of the LORD and set me down in the middle of the valley; and it was full of bones. 2 And he led me around among them, and behold, there were very many on the surface of the valley, and behold, they were very dry. 3 And he said to me, "Son of man, can these bones live?" And I answered, "O Lord GOD, you know." 4 Then he said to me, "Prophesy over these bones, and say to them, O dry bones, hear the word of the LORD. 5 Thus says the Lord GOD to these bones: Behold, I will cause breath to enter you, and you shall live. 6 And I will lay sinews upon you, and will cause flesh to come upon you, and cover you with skin, and put breath in you, and you shall live, and you shall know that I am the LORD."
- Afterwards, write a list of attributes you would like to see in your partner so that when you pray for him/her, you can begin to speak them prophetically as though they already are.

PRAYER

Father, we thank You for blessing us with each other. Thank You, Lord for my wife/husband who is a great partner, who is supportive, encouraging, reassuring, validating, kind, loving, considerate, gentle, thoughtful, helpful and faithful. Father, thank You for giving us Your very best, for blessing our marriage and for watching over us. In Jesus' name, we pray. Amen.

'We have heard the saying, "An apple a day keeps the doctor away". Likewise, the couple that prays together stays together.' p. 115

Day 26

The Weapons of Our Warfare

2 CORINTHIANS 10: 3-6

3 For though we walk in the flesh, we are not waging war according to the flesh. 4 For the weapons of our warfare are not of the flesh but have divine power to destroy strongholds. 5 We destroy arguments and every lofty opinion raised against the knowledge of God, and take every thought captive to obey Christ, 6 being ready to punish every disobedience, when your obedience is complete.

REFLECTION

Your partner is not your adversary. I will repeat this for emphasis. Your husband is not your enemy. Your wife is not your enemy. But you do have a mutual enemy. "Be sober-minded; be watchful. Your adversary the devil prowls around like a roaring lion, seeking someone to devour" (1 Peter 5: 8). When you fail to recognize who your enemy is you fall for the tricks of your enemy who causes you to misunderstand the words and actions of your spouse. Consider the number of times, you make an innocent comment to your spouse and are surprised by the anger that your comment generated. For example, you said,

"Are you cooking fish again today?" Meaning, "I enjoyed the fish you cooked yesterday". However, at that very moment, your wife begins to entertain thoughts such as, "He is always criticizing you! He did not like your fish yesterday and lied when he said he did! He does not appreciate the sacrifice that you are making for him! YOUR MARRIAGE IS NOT WORKING!"

The enemy does not use the same strategies with all couple's but, having been around for a long time, is deliberate in selecting his timing and methods for best results. Many of you are stuck in unhelpful behavioral patterns hurting each other again and again when you don't desire to do so. It's time to unite against your common enemy. The weapons that will be most effective aren't your carnal/ physical weapons. You have already gone to your friends to complain about your husband and yet this has not been helpful beyond the temporary relief you've gotten from venting. Walking out of the house every time your wife "nags" you isn't working either. Typically, you return home to either resume arguing or to nurse the feelings of guilt about not being the husband you truly desire to be.

Do your part to take responsibility for your words and your actions while interacting with your spouse, humble your selves before God and each other, then fight for your marriage on your knees by praying to God and trusting that He will fight on your behalf. 2 Chronicles 7: 14 states that, "if my people who are called by my name humble themselves, and pray and seek my face and turn from their wicked ways, then I will hear from heaven and will forgive their sin and heal their land". God will not only heal your land. He will also heal your marriage.

COUPLE ENRICHMENT EXERCISE

Practice taking a timeout to pray when you catch yourself becoming defensive with your partner. Agree on the following process beforehand as the measure you will take to handle conflict that appears to be escalating:

- During conversation with each other you begin to feel angry or stressed.
- One or both of you should indicate the need for a time out. You could create a code word or phrase that you both agree to that will be a reminder for you.
- Hold each other's hand and pray asking God to help you to overcome and to refrain from hurting each other.

PRAYER

Father, You are our defense. We know that we wrestle not against each other, but against the wicked one whose intent is to kill, steal and destroy. Teach us to submit to each other in humility. Remind us that our battle is not a physical battle and teach us how to fight using our spiritual weapons. Father, cover us with Your spiritual armor. Remind us that we are more than conquerors in You. Grant us the resolve to brandish our shield of faith to withstand the fiery darts of the enemy on our marriage, and teach us to use your Word as our sure defense. In Jesus' name, we pray. Amen.

Day 27

It's HARD WORK!

COLOSSIANS 3: 23-24

23 Whatever you do, work heartily, as for the Lord and not for men, 24 knowing that from the Lord you will receive the inheritance as your reward. You are serving the Lord Christ.

REFLECTION

Thirteen years ago I attended a wedding and I felt sorry for the couple who had to endure one speaker after another bemoan the fact that marriage is HARD WORK! Yet, this warning was necessary because many couples are not adequately prepared for the reality of marriage. The misconception is that, "If we were truly meant to be together it would not be this hard". Having this immature perspective on marriage is a recipe for disaster. One must keep in mind that marriage is, in reality, a union between two imperfect people who are prone to errors, emotional fluctuations, and the effects of life events that disrupt their personal equilibrium. A prudent person who enrolls in a challenging math class about which they were forewarned would make significant adjustments to ensure that they can meet the demands. Likewise, marriage requires considerable preparation.

COUPLE ENRICHMENT EXERCISE

There are practical things that couples MUST do to nurture their marriage and increase their chance of success. Consider the following list and work at incorporating them into your daily routine:

- Spend time together in private
- Have conversations with each other that are respectful yet open and honest
- Have regular sexual relations with each other
- Engage in shared activities that allow you to have fun together
- Pray together
- Remain accountable to God and trusted mentors especially a couple that is more mature than yourselves
- Support each other's interests and leisure activities
- And support each other’s ministry as you advance the Kingdom of God

PRAYER

Father, instill a desire within us to WORK HARD at our marriage. Grant us the right attitude that will increase our chance of success. Grant within us a positive mindset that drives us to work through the nuances and disturbances in our daily lives. Teach us to celebrate the small things and to work together on the things we need to do to improve our relationship. Father, there are things that will often disturb us and at times derail us, but we know we can trust in your sovereignty. We know you specialize in the impossible, so equip us in every way possible to remain focused on being proactive to keep our marriage above reproach. In Jesus' name, we pray. Amen.

"Thirteen years ago I attended a wedding and I felt sorry for the couple who had to endure one speaker after another bemoan the fact that marriage is HARD WORK! Yet, this warning was necessary because many couples are not adequately prepared for the reality of marriage." p. 123

Day 28

But With God All Things Are Possible

MARK 10: 2-12

2 And Pharisees came up and in order to test him asked, "Is it lawful for a man to divorce his wife?" 3 He answered them, "What did Moses command you?" 4 They said, "Moses allowed a man to write a certificate of divorce and to send her away."5 And Jesus said to them, "Because of your hardness of heart he wrote you this commandment. 6 But from the beginning of creation, 'God made them male and female.' 7 'Therefore a man shall leave his father and mother and hold fast to his wife, 8 and the two shall become one flesh.' So they are no longer two but one flesh. 9 What therefore God has joined together, let not man separate." 10 And in the house the disciples asked him again about this matter. 11 And he said to them, "Whoever divorces his wife and marries another commits adultery against her, 12 and if she divorces her husband and marries another, she commits adultery."

REFLECTION

You have done all that is within your power and yet divorce seems to be inevitable. Who could blame you? There is adultery, there is abuse, you have not slept in the same bed for years, and you detest each other… even so, nothing is impossible for God.

The book of Exodus tells the history of God's deliverance of the Nation of Israel. The children of Israel were in captivity for over 400 years when God sent Moses to instruct Pharaoh to let his people go. It took ten attempts which included the demonstration of signs and wonders for Pharaoh to release his captives. No sooner had he released them than he changed his mind and proceeded to hunt them down driving fear into their hearts. The impossible was unfolding as God prepared to demonstrate his omnipotence through one of the greatest miracles recorded in the Bible. As a prelude to this miracle, the Israelite's were trapped between the Red Sea and their enemies.

If you read the book of Exodus you might be surprised or perhaps even confused when you recognize that God was in complete control. In fact, the Bible teaches us that God hardened pharaoh's heart. Exodus 4:21 states, And the Lord said to Moses, "When you go back to Egypt, see that you do before Pharaoh all the miracles that I have put in your power. But I will harden his heart, so that he will not let the people go." What? Are you misunderstanding and misrepresenting scripture? Let's put it this way. That experience can easily be likened to the experience of Jesus deliberately showing up four days late and making sure that Lazarus was really dead (John 11). Now, you are really taking it too far. No, I'm not. I could go on and on and on, but I will get back to the original point.

If Pharaoh had released the children of Israel after the first encounter with Moses, we would have no idea that God's deliverance is sure. Not only is it sure, but God will part the sea and raise the dead if that's what is necessary according to His Will. God often allows us to get to the brink of disaster before he steps in and delivers us. The simplest way of making sense of this is that it's through the unfolding of the process, coming to terms with the impossible, then experiencing God's power and might that we really begin to recognize who God really is. Furthermore, subsequent to our deliverance we also become compelling witnesses to others of who God is.

Abuse in any form should never be tolerated and for that reason, there are circumstances in which a controlled separation from an abusive partner is the best course of action. This allows partners to seek intervention, gain necessary support and work through root issues to prevent future occurrences.

With that said, I am saying to you that the God who is able to part the Red Sea, allowing his children to walk across the expanse on dry land before drowning their enemy, and the God who raised a man from the grave who had already been dead for four days, is more than able to save your marriage. In fact, He will resurrect your dead marriage and

He will make a way for you to cross the red sea. Is there anything too hard for our God?

COUPLE ENRICHMENT EXERCISE

If you forget what God has done in your past, it will continue to be challenging to trust Him in the present. Begin to consider and record what God has done in your lives and watch your Faith Grow!

PRAYER

Father, we know that our thoughts are not your thoughts and our ways are not your ways. The impossible things that are blocking our progress in our marriage are not too hard for you to change! Father, rather than choose divorce, we surrender our marriage to you and pray that Your Will be done. Lord, command your angels concerning our marriage to minister to our hurts and to heal our hearts. We believe that you are the Resurrection and Life so we ask you to restore us and revive us. Breathe on us Lord and give us new life. We accept by faith that, as we choose to surrender to you, you will save our marriage for Your Glory and Honour. In Jesus' name, we pray. Amen.

Day 29

My Pledge

JOSHUA 24:15

And if it is evil in your eyes to serve the Lord, choose this day whom you will serve, whether the gods your fathers served in the region beyond the River, or the gods of the Amorites in whose land you dwell. But as for me and my house, we will serve the Lord.

REFLECTION

When you stood with your spouse at the altar, you made a covenant not just with your spouse but more importantly, with God. Is it a small matter to break a covenant? You made promises to God and you are accountable to Him for those promises.

In these specific words or others, you made the following promise:
"I, ___, take you, ___, for my lawful wife/husband, to have and to hold from this day forward, for better, for worse, for richer, for poorer, in sickness and health, until death do us part."

God will not release you from this covenant simply because you no longer love each other. He is, however, faithful and merciful and he is a God who is touched by your infirmities. Hebrews 4: 14-16 commands us to hold fast our confession:

“14 Since then we have a great high priest who has passed through the heavens, Jesus, the Son of God, let us hold fast our confession. 15 For we do not have a high priest who is unable to sympathize with our weaknesses, but one who in every respect has been tempted as we are, yet without sin. 16 Let us then with confidence draw near to the throne of grace, that we may receive mercy and find grace to help in time of need.”

You have not tried EVERYTHING! When I persisted in breaking my covenant with my husband/ with God, God gave me a glimpse of my future without His chosen husband in it. If I had persisted in looking for love in places outside of my Heavenly Father, I would have inevitably discovered that what I was looking for is an illusion; a lie from the adversary. Furthermore, my husband would have eventually healed and moved on without me. God also changed my heart and enabled me to see that Norman is an amazing husband and father. He is imperfect. He is not Jesus Christ; but, he is *God's Best Husband* for me. Therefore, I still choose to take God at His word. I also submit myself to His refining process as he continuously moulds and shapes me into *His Best Wife* for Norman. Today, I am grateful that I now have the opportunity to see the great potential that God placed in the husband he chose for me.

This is your 29th Day of the journey and I have an important question for you. Will you also give God a chance to change your heart and to show you that He will make your marriage into the marriage he intended when he placed you with your spouse?

COUPLE ENRICHMENT EXERCISE

Now it's time for you to renew your covenant with your spouse and with God. It doesn't matter that it's not your 5th, 10th, 15th, 25th, 30th, 50th, or 75th Anniversary. To do it God's way is to go all in. Therefore, it is important that you stand with each other before God and pledge your renewed commitment to each other and to your Heavenly Father.
You might even consider having an official ceremony with your pastor and with other witnesses, but remember that the size of your ceremony is not salient.

In addition to your vows outlined above, you are further pledging the following to each other and to God:

1. Lord, we pledge to continuously approach Your Throne of Grace as a couple.
2. We pledge to humble ourselves and allow You to show us our hearts so that You will mould us into the image of Your Son.
3. We pledge to repent as soon as Your Holy Spirit convicts us of our sins so that You will continually cleanse us.

4. We pledge to offer our marriage to You as a sacrifice, and to submit to Your Will.
5. We pledge to follow Jesus' Example of a marriage ordained by You.
6. We pledge to continually ask You to break our walls down so that the adversary has no opportunity to devour us.
7. We pledge to accept by faith that Your Grace is Sufficient for us.
8. We pledge to continually seek You individually so that You will fill us with Your living water and nourish us with Your bread of life.
9. Lord, we pledge to come before You and to submit ourselves so that You can help us to understand our role in our marriage, and enable us to be consistent in carrying our joint responsibilities.
10. We pledge to accept our dependence on each other and on You.
11. We pledge to take You at Your word that as we continue to seek You together, You will change our hearts so that we will love each other unconditionally.
12. We pledge that we will invest our time in doing the things we did at the beginning of our relationship that first caused us to fall in love with each other.
13. We pledge to work at becoming the best husband and wife we could ever be to each other.
14. We pledge to work hard at enhancing each other's lives.

15. We pledge to try new behaviors in order to grow as a couple.
16. We pledge to do practical things to solve our problems in addition to the time we spend talking about them.
17. We pledge to learn about each other by asking about and supporting each other's interests.
18. We pledge to practice providing clear and specific feedback concerning how we are being affected by each other.
19. We pledge to accept and incorporate the feedback we receive from each other to increase our level of satisfaction in our marriage.
20. We pledge to continue working at remaining non-defensive by sincerely telling each other what we could do to make improvements in our marriage.
21. We pledge to try new shared activities regularly to keep our marriage fresh and exciting.
22. We pledge to keep Christ at the center of our marriage to ensure that our foundation remains solid.
23. We pledge to seek refuge in You and to remain under Your shadow.
24. We pledge to fight our battles on our knees rather than fight each other.
25. And we pledge to take You at Your word that nothing is impossible for You.

PRAYER

Father, we pledge our allegiance to You and to each other. We choose to place each other's needs above our own and to break all connections with other persons that violate our covenant with you and with each other. Father, help us to honour our vows. Lord, as we hold each other's hands and gaze at each other's face, we choose this day that our house will serve You. In Jesus' name, we pray. Amen.

Day 30

Our Marriage in 1, 5 & 10 Years

PROVERBS 19: 20-21
20 Listen to advice and accept discipline, and at the end you will be counted among the wise. 21 Many are the plans in a person's heart, but it is the LORD's purpose that prevails.

REFLECTION
God knows the future. He knows the plans he has for you individually and as a couple. How amazing is it to rest in the assurance that the one in whom you put your trust is the only one that can guarantee your future? We are approaching the end of this 30-Day journey and yet it is only the beginning for you.

Hebrews 4: 12 teaches that "the word of God is living and active, sharper than any two-edged sword, piercing to the division of soul and of spirit, of joints and of marrow, and discerning the thoughts and intentions of the heart." You have been pushed way beyond your comfort zone throughout this journey. You have been challenged by some hard to accept truths and now you are making your way down the home stretch… the last 50 meters in the race for your Best Marriage.

Begin to petition God for a deeper understanding of your purpose as a couple and the marriage he desires for you to have 1 year, 5 years and 10 years from today. Write it down and believe that His word will not return to him empty, but will accomplish that which he purposed.

COUPLE ENRICHMENT EXERCISE

Spend some time in your Secret Space and pray concerning God's future for your marriage. Afterward, sit with each other and write what he reveals. You may not yet understand how God speaks to you, but accept by faith that as you put pen to paper, what comes to the forefront is what He intends for you to become aware of:

God's Picture of My Marriage 1-Year from Today

God's Picture of My Marriage 5-Years from Today

God's Picture of My Marriage 10-Years from Today

PRAYER

Father, the restoration journey for our marriage was not an easy one. You have allowed us to see your straight and narrow path and you have declared your expectations concerning our marriage. As we reflect on your Word we have seen our faults and our flaws. We have seen the strengths and weakness in ourselves and each other and we desire to love each other as Christ loves His Church. Teach us to be wise and to accept correction. Father, thank you for showing us what a healthy and harmonious relationship should look like. Be with us in our Secret Space as we abide under your shadow. We lift our hands to you in adoration! You are a Holy God and You are worthy of honour and praise. Hallelujah!!! Amen and Amen.

My Prayer for Your Marriage

Heavenly Father, I stand in the gap for this couple who, like Daniel, has purposed in their hearts to not defile themselves with the delicacies of the society in which they live. I pray that You will command Your angels concerning their marriage. I pray for Your favor in their finances. I pray that You will bless the fruit of their loins. I pray that You will draw their hearts to You. I pray that You will expose the lies of the adversary concerning their marriage. Lord, I pray that You will minister peace and harmony in their home, and I pray that You will be present in the Secret Space they now share with You. Lord, I am believing You for all this and for more concerning Your children. In Jesus' beautiful and precious name I pray. Amen

"Lord, I pray that You will minister peace and harmony in their home, and I pray that You will be present in the Secret Space they now share with You." p. 143

Farewell

You have come a long way over the past 30 days and I commend you for your courage. This was not easy for you, yet you persevered and pushed yourself through the discomfort and the pain. I encourage you to trust in the Lord with all your heart and refrain from leaning on your own understanding. Marriage is HARD WORK! If you doubt that do consider the marriages you see in the society, social and popular media. It is easy to start most things in life but very few people finish well. You were never meant to do it alone. God intended from the beginning to be intimately involved in your daily experiences. Furthermore, it is in your weaknesses that you come to find grace in the arms of God as His power is perfected in those weaknesses. May God bless and keep your marriage by doing exceedingly, abundantly above all that you could ask or think, according to the power of God that works in you. To Him be glory in the Church by Christ Jesus to all generations, forever and ever. Amen.

"Each day's Devotion includes: The passage of Scripture that is the focal point for the day; Reflections in which the author teaches concerning a specific aspect of marriage, and integrates the lesson with the passages of Scripture highlighted; Couple Enrichment Exercises that provide couples with an opportunity to practice what they have learned that day; and finally a written Prayer for the couple to petition God concerning their marriage based on the specific need identified in the Reflection and Couple Enrichment Exercises." p. xv